"Bill Butterworth makes me laugh, but more importantly he makes me think. Bill is much more than an inspirational speaker....He is a locomotive of energy....No wonder I like him so much."

> —JACK KEMP, former vice presidential candidate and
> founder and chairman of Kemp Partners

"We are impressed with Bill's style, content, and ability to connect with the audience. He's an outstanding communicator—versatile in approach and content."

> —WALT DISNEY COMPANY

"Our entire management team enjoys how appropriate the subject of work-life balance is for the organization."

> —FORD MOTOR COMPANY

"In a hard-charging business environment it's difficult to maintain perspective; Bill Butterworth's ideas on balance are very appropriate."

> —AMERICAN EXPRESS

"A home run! The mix of humor and message was just what we hoped for."

> —BANK OF AMERICA

"Wonderful! Wow!"

"Bill Butterworth is terrific on the subject of work-life balance. He brings joy and laughter to senior executives; I would recommend him to any group seeking to improve morale or simply to develop key members' leadership skills."

"Bill is dynamite! He has the rare ability to relax his audience with humor, followed by a powerful, riveting message driven home forcefully."

"An outstanding message. Bill Butterworth is helping our employees lead balanced lives."

"Bill Butterworth's contributions helped kick us into high gear! He was the highest-rated speaker of our entire conference...a smashing success!"

"Fantastic! Bill Butterworth put smiles on our faces, touched our hearts, and reminded us of what is really important in life."

"Bill Butterworth's insight into management and corporate relations regarding employer-employee teamwork and business-to-client relationships assisted my firm to grow 25 percent in one year versus the projected 12 percent. I highly recommend Bill's strategies to every CEO. His insight into how people relate to each other is second to none!"

—HAR-BRO INCORPORATED

"Bill's time with our company was the best motivational experience we've had. He articulated our vision and balanced it with values we respect."

—MORTON INDUSTRIAL GROUP

"Perfect mix of humor and message. How can we possibly thank Bill Butterworth enough!"

—CALIFORNIA CREDIT UNION LEAGUE

"Bill's blend of humor, insight, and storytelling left us with unforgettable mental pictures of how to manage change."

—TRANZACT SYSTEMS

"Bill Butterworth keeps us on the edge of our seats. The issue of balance between our obligations to family, work, and personal time is important; rarely has that message been offered with such energy or received with such enthusiasm. Bill's message is timely and presented in such a way that resonates."

—COUNCIL OF ALUMNI ASSOCIATION EXECUTIVES

"Bill Butterworth's participation and contribution are definitely a key factor to success. His enthusiasm, sense of humor, and ability to involve the audience—all wonderful!"

    —KNOTT'S BERRY FARM

"Bill has given us many points to consider. Time with him seems like time shared with a longtime friend. He brings humor and personality."

    —DEUTSCHE FINANCIAL SERVICES

"A 10 in every way. Bill is interesting, amusing, and insightful, and his ideas go a long way in helping our membership."

    —MEETING PROFESSIONALS INTERNATIONAL

"Great style. Bill Butterworth had us in the palm of his hand and left us feeling happy, satisfied, and with a new outlook on life!"

    —AIMS LOGISTICS

"Outstanding! Bill is super!"

    —GULF POWER

"Bill's evaluations were overwhelmingly positive, and many cited his presentation as the conference highlight!"

    —NATIONAL ASSOCIATION OF CATERING EXECUTIVES

"Outstanding presentation…terrific."

    —ELECTRICAL APPARATUS SERVICE ASSOCIATION

on-the-fly guide to...

Balancing
Work
&Life

on-the-fly guide to...

Balancing
Work
& Life

Bill Butterworth

CURRENCY

DOUBLEDAY

New York London Toronto Sydney Auckland

Published in association with the literary agency of Alive Communications, Inc., 7680 Goddard Street, Suite 200, Colorado Springs, Colorado 80290, www.alivecommunications.com

Library of Congress Cataloging-in-Publication Data
Butterworth, Bill.
 On-the-fly guide to—balancing work and life / Bill Butterworth.—1st ed.
       p. cm.
 Includes bibliographical references.
 1. Work and family.   2. Conduct of life.   I. Title: Balancing work and life.   II. Title.
 HD4904.25.B88 2006
 650.1—dc22   2006001035

ISBN-13: 978-0-385-51968-7
ISBN-10: 0-385-51968-0

Printed in the United States of America

Special Sales
Currency Books are available at special discounts for bulk purchases for sales promotions or premiums. Special editions, including personalized covers, excerpts of existing books, and corporate imprints, can be created in large quantities for special needs. For more information, write to Special Markets, Currency Books, specialmarkets@randomhouse.com

10 9 8 7 6 5 4 3

First Edition

For Kathi

Love with wings

Contents

Acknowledgments

A book is always a collaborative effort. Therefore, I have many people to thank who have invested in my life. In countless ways they have made a great contribution to this book.

Don Pape sparked my creative fire with the original idea for a series entitled "On-the-Fly." As my literary agent and friend, he has always been willing to listen to my ramblings. He deserves an extra pat on the back for being so patient with me. All the folks at Alive Communications are fantastic, and I owe a special debt of gratitude to *Lee Hough.*

The people at Doubleday have been wonderfully kind to me. I am so indebted to *Michael Palgon, Roger Scholl,* and *Sarah Rainone* for their loving care in handling this project.

The gang at WaterBrook Press is amazing. I have spent a fair amount of time with them, and they are still publishing me! To name a few: *Steve Cobb, Dudley Delffs, Mick Silva, Jessica Barnes, Carol Bartley, Brian McGinley, Ginia Hairston, Jan Walker, Kevin Hallwyler, Lori Addicott, Joel Kneedler, Leah McMahan,* and *Alice Crider* are all part of one fantastic team.

I have wonderful friends in my life. I am so grateful to people like *Lee* and *Leslie Strobel, Joe* and *Molly Davis, Mike* and *Marcia Scott, Ron* and *Kay Nelson, Bob* and *Barb Ludwig, Gary* and *Linda Bender, Jim* and *Ines Franklin, Al* and *Anita Manley, Val* and *Linda*

Giannini, Todd and *Cheryl Jensen, Ruben* and *Trish Guzman,* and *Ken* and *Judy Gire* for their valuable contributions on a regular basis.

Many business leaders have believed in me from the start, and I must acknowledge their constant insight and encouragement. I know I will miss some, but special thanks to *Bill Morton, Mike Sime, Mike Regan, Mark Zoradi, Bill Coyne, Brad Quayle, Dave Nelson, Dee Tolles, Dave Stone, Dan Lungren, Joe Ahern, Bob Buford, John Pearson, Tim Cass, Ralph Jones, Rich Caturano, Jim Gwinn, Keith Harrell, Mark Thomas, Rick Warren, Bob Harron, Bill Hybels, Jon Singley, Ron Whitmill, Joe Belew,* and *Mark Laudeman.*

I also want to thank all the speakers' bureaus that have faithfully represented me over the years. I am greatly indebted to you, not just for the business, but also for your friendship.

My children (and now grandchildren) have hung in with me through good times and bad. You are my great treasure. Thank you for all you have taught me.

And finally, my dear wife, *Kathi.* You know all about me and choose to live with me anyway. Thanks so very much. You're amazing.

One

What I Know About Balance
I Learned on the Track Team

I can describe my entire childhood in one run-on sentence: I weighed back *then* what I weigh *now* and I was four feet shorter and my last name was Butterworth.

Can you visualize it? It's not a very pretty picture.

Like everyone else, I quickly observed that our school had a group of kids who really ran the place. They were the cool ones. In the school I went to, just outside Philadelphia, the cool kids were the athletes. I naively grew up thinking all athletes were cool, but that is not necessarily so. It could be that you went to a school where the band was tough or the chess club ruled. But in my hometown it was the jocks, and I wanted to be just like them. Yet there weren't many coaches anxious for me to join their team.

I can remember, however, the first time the football coach laid eyes on me. He took one look at my size and began to drool with animal anticipation. "Butterworth," he barked, "if I could just get you on my offensive line, my strategy would be simple. I'd have you hike the ball and roll over. The defensive line would be lost for hours. They wouldn't even know what field they were playing on! We could score at will."

Naturally excited at the prospect, I went home to tell my parents the good news that the football coach not only wanted me, but he wanted me badly. I recall being heartbroken when my folks said I couldn't play football. "I don't want to see my 'little Billy' [my first oxymoron] getting hurt," my overprotective mother said.

I was no medical doctor, but I honestly believed that, because of the way I was built, it was physically impossible for me to get hurt. There was so much padding on my body, it would have been a miracle if someone could have found something hard enough to break—unless there is an ailment known as strained cellulite.

But football was out of the question.

I was crushed.

So, in a complete admission of failure, I joined the marching band. It was a Fat Kid Fraternity, where the common bond was the pain of rejection. There I was, taking up the entire back three rows of the marching band, watching the cool kids instead of being one.

But that all changed one day after a social studies class. "Butterworth, I want to see you after class," my teacher announced as the bell was about to ring. I slowly walked to the front of the room like a man being led to the gallows, wondering what I possibly could have done. I was stumped, for I worked hard to keep my nose clean at school.

Mr. Warren greeted me warmly. "Butterworth, have you ever considered going out for the school's track team?" he inquired.

I was stunned. *Gee, kids make fun of me all the time,* I thought. *Now teachers are asking me to stay after class for a little one-on-one heckling.* But I maintained a positive demeanor. After all, this man was responsible for my grade in social studies, so I didn't dare come off disrespectful in any way. I swallowed hard and squeaked out the only response I could think of:

"Sir, I don't think I'm very fast."

Mr. Warren held back a chuckle. "Son, I wasn't thinking of having you run." He paused while I let out a sigh of relief. "There are other parts to a track team," he continued. "There are the field events. I think you'd be very effective in the weightman events."

"Weightman events?"

"The shot put, Butterworth. The big steel ball that you place under your chin. You don't throw it; you put it." He illustrated the motion by bringing his hand from his chin out to its full extension.

"I see."

"And then there's the discus, Butterworth. You know—the plate- or saucer-looking thing that you throw. Surely you've seen the famous statue of the discus thrower, haven't you, Butterworth?"

My face turned ashen.

"Relax, Butterworth, relax. They wear clothes now when they throw it."

"Oh."

"Ask your mom and dad if you can come out for the team," Mr. Warren suggested. "We've got a place waiting for you."

I went home that evening with absolutely no expectation of a positive response. I felt that my parents were anti-sports and track would be treated no differently than football. I was braced for more despair. It was painful enough being a fat kid, but add to it parents who protest the coolest activity in school, and you've got all the ingredients of a defeated childhood. So imagine my complete surprise when I threw the question out and was met with encouragement.

"That sounds like a great idea!" my parents replied. They liked the idea of a noncontact sport. I could throw the shot put and the discus to my heart's content. (Although I do remember having to sign a form promising my parents I would not try to *catch* these implements after they were thrown.)

Overnight I was transformed from a member of the marching band to BILL BUTTERWORTH—ATHLETE. I liked the way that looked and sounded. I finally felt cool.

In the northeastern part of the country, where I grew up, track is a two-season sport. Winter track takes place indoors, and spring track is outside. I quickly discovered that if you are a weightman, winter track means going into a tiny—and smelly—room off the boys' gym and lifting weights. This continues until spring, when you are finally allowed to go outside. Weightmen love the spring.

All humility aside, there were certain parts of this weightman scene in which I excelled. Mainly, I had great form. I knew how to slide across the circle, crouched low, and then, at just the precise moment, *explode* with great intensity (and a primitive grunt) in order to throw the shot put a mile. In the same way, I knew how to spin around through the circle for the discus throw, like a spring unwinding. I knew how to uncoil and, once again, *explode* at the optimum moment of release.

Yes, my form was outstanding…especially without the implements.

It was when I actually had to throw the darn things that it all unraveled. You see, I had no strength. Even with my perfect form, great slides and spins, and intense *explosion,* neither the shot put nor the discus went any distance when I threw it.

I was the only guy they measured with a ruler.

But I refused to become discouraged. I was one of the cool guys, and that's what mattered most. I even remember the day I discovered how they keep score in a track meet. Points are awarded to those who come in first, second, or third. I did a little mental math and realized that I was the *fifth* man on my own team. That meant I would never score any points unless the opposition forfeited and malaria worked its way through our squad. But a chance to score points came up in a rather unusual circumstance.

As I was growing up, my parents saw to it that I was in church every Sunday. At the time, we went to a church that I would describe as "socially active." By that I mean they had sporting events for every taste. They had church flag football in the fall, church basketball in the winter, and church softball in the spring. But they went far beyond those conventional contests. We had all-church boccie ball, all-church canasta, all-church darts—we had all the bases covered, so to speak.

One spring the question was raised: "There's a certain sport in which we've never participated. How about an all-church track meet?"

I was beside myself with exhilaration. "Yes, yes, we must have an all-church track meet!" In my head, I couldn't help but conclude, *I'll finally score some points in a track meet. I'll mop up on these church wimps!*

The day of the all-church track meet arrived on a lovely spring Saturday with the trees budding and the birds singing. Since our church was hosting the event, we held it at the local public high-school track, meaning I was right at home in the shot put and discus circles. It was my turf.

As the weightmen arrived, it was quickly apparent that I was the only one with any formal training in these events. I used this to my advantage, going through what every athlete knows as his "pre-meet psych-out" of the opposition. I began by demonstrating my form in the circle (without using the shot or discus) and sat back to listen to the oohs and the aahs of my competitors, who had never even picked up a weightman implement, let alone worked on the form necessary to be a champion. I put on quite a show.

Then the time came to actually compete. As usual, my form was impeccable. And, as usual, the implements went nowhere. What transpired was the height of embarrassment for a seasoned track man like me. These guys—these *church* guys—who had never even seen a shot put or a discus before threw them like they were born with one in their bassinet. When the dust settled, the results were all too familiar.

I hadn't placed in either event.

My teammates came over as their events concluded. I was sitting on the side of the circle, utterly dejected, contemplating if life was worth living.

"How did you do?" they asked. "Did you win the shot put?"

I just looked down and shook my head.

"Second or third?"

"No."

"How about the discus? That's really your event, isn't it? Did you win?"

"No."

"Second or third?"

"No." With tears in my eyes, I looked up at my teammates and choked out, "I can't believe it. I didn't score any points!"

The awkward silence was suddenly broken by another teammate who had just run over from the track. He had heard the end of our discussion, and he quickly chimed in, "Well, 'Mr. Butterworth—athlete,' this must be your lucky day, because it looks like you're gonna get another chance!"

"What do you mean?"

"Well, the next event over on the track is the 440. Bobby is supposed to run it, but he just pulled a muscle in the 220. The rules state that each member of the team can compete in three events. You are the only guy on the team to compete in just two, so you're going to run a 440!"

At this point, my teammates were anxiously taking off my shoes and replacing them with running spikes. These shoes were light as feathers, with the spikes on the front of the sole, making you feel as if you needed to stand on your toes. Once I had the spikes on, the oddest feeling crept over me... *I felt fast!*

It made no sense. Here I was, the size of a mid-Atlantic state, and I had the feeling that I was speedy. Something was wrong with this picture.

But the whole thing happened so quickly I didn't have time to think. Before I knew it, my teammates had me over to the track, and I had received my lane assignment (I was in lanes four, five, and six, as I recall). And the next thing I knew—bang!—the gun went off, signaling the beginning of the race.

As I took off from the starting line, I was suddenly overtaken with panic. I realized there were a million questions about this race that I had neglected to ask, most notably, *What is the strategy for running a 440?* Balance is like any other endeavor in our life. It's not going to happen if we don't get intentional about it. We need a strategy, or a plan, put in place if it's going to work.

I looked over to the sidelines, making eye contact with my teammates. It was one of those magical moments when there is a silent communication among men. No words had to be spoken, for the question was clearly written all over my pained face. In response, a teammate yelled a strategy to me. It was a brief sentence, yet it is one I can still hear today. As a matter of fact, I still wake up at night in the middle of a nightmare, hearing these same words. He yelled:

"It's only a lap!"

I let that sink in for a second. *It's only a lap.* I have now come to equate that phrase with others like "It's only terminal."

Nonetheless, I had precious little time to mull this over in my mind. I quickly ascertained that the keyword in that strategy was the word *only*. *It's only one lap around the football field. That's all,* I reassured myself. With that in mind, I settled on the strategy that would take me through this race.

It must be a sprint, I concluded.

So I took off. Most of us have seen this type of race conducted at our high-school tracks. The starting point of the race is the part of the track by the fifty-yard line on the home side of the field. That will also serve as the finish line so that the winner can break the tape in front of the maximum number of cheering fans.

For the first 110 yards down the track toward the goalpost, I ran all out. In doing so, I was just behind the runner who was in the lead at that point. It never dawned on me that he was saving a little energy for the rest of the race. I pushed a little harder, and by the time we were 110 yards into it, I was tied with him for first place!

This did a lot for my confidence. I decided that I would set another short-term goal (my first goal had been to run 110 yards and *still be standing*). This second goal was a greater reach for me: be the sole possessor of first place by the race's halfway point. I gave it everything I had. Frankly, people still comment to me that they have never seen a fat boy move so fast. The tonnage was really hauling.

Sure enough, by the time I crossed the fifty-yard line on the visitors' side of the field, first place was all mine! I was moving on sheer adrenaline at this point. I recall thinking to myself, *This is unbelievable! All that time slaving away at the shot put and discus circle, when the truth is I'm a runner!* This was quite some time before the release of the film *Chariots of Fire;* otherwise, I am certain the orchestra would have swelled with the movie theme at this point in the race. I would have thrown my head back, run barefoot, and started speaking with a Scottish accent!

As I headed toward the other goalpost, I was in a state of euphoria. I decided that my third goal, upon reaching the 330-yard mark, was to have fully prepared my remarks for when I accepted the gold medal at the finish line. ("I want to thank everyone who made this win possible—my mom, my dad, my coach, all the little people behind the scenes," etc.)

By the time I arrived at those goalposts, I had a rather substantial lead. But that is where *it* happened—at the 330-yard mark of the race. Exactly what was "it"? Let me answer this way...

From this point on in the story, I must tell it to you as it was later told to me.

Something happened to me at 330 yards. I have been told by serious runners since then that I "hit the wall." I had no concept of what was going on at the time, however. I remember feeling as though two guys had run up behind me and each had stuck a hypodermic needle in my buns. One needle was filled with battery acid, because every part of my body was stinging in unparalleled pain. The other needle was filled with Jell-O, because my entire body had gone soft, even the parts that were previously hard.

By this point, I was running in a very unorthodox manner. Here I was, the size of Utah, weaving and swaying, threatening to drop at any second. Looking back, I realize that I was the only guy within five miles of the track who didn't understand what was about to happen.

Fat Boy was going down.

My teammates, embarrassingly aware of what was about to transpire, were screaming at me, "Fall in, fall in!" By that they meant fall *in* toward the football field, since it was obvious that the big guy was going to take a tumble. That way, I could roll around in the grass infield for hours without disturbing anyone. If, however, I fell *out*, I would still be on the track, creating a natural hazard, vulnerable to whatever was behind me. Plus, it would take a crane to remove me.

By now I was out of my mind. There were no brain cells functioning in my cranial cavity. I was ready to drop, and everyone knew it. The only question was, would I fall in or out?

Unable to go another step, I fell.

Out.

Rolling around on the track, I was crying and sweating and eating black cinders that tasted like death. I was in excruciating pain—the outer, physical variety. *I've never felt so bad!* I thought. *Nothing could be any worse!*

Suddenly I heard the rumble of runners' feet behind me. What couldn't get worse was about to.

"How are we supposed to get around this?" a runner grumbled as the other runners soon came upon the same blockade of fat.

"Yeah, what is this, a steeplechase?" chimed in another.

I was so large that no one wanted to take the extra seconds to run around me, so they decided to scale me, adding blood to my sweat and tears. Their spikes tore away at the pounds that had padded me so well for so many years. They ran over me and went on to finish the race, leaving me 110 yards behind, rolling around like a giant glob of cookie dough.

I'll never forget that race as long as I live.

It's such an old metaphor, it is axiomatic: life is like a race. I have come to embrace that metaphor more fully as time has gone by. As I grew into adulthood, especially with the addition of the vocational element to my life, I saw even more clearly that many of the aspects I experienced as a "runner" were now a part of my everyday life. So if life is like a race (and I've discovered it is), then this is perhaps the most significant question that must be addressed:

What kind of race am I running?

Without getting into too much technical track jargon, there are basically two types of races—*long* ones and *short* ones.

Short races are known as sprints. A sprint is characterized by speed and quickness. It's the race that you'll miss if you turn your head.

Ask my five kids about sprints. They know. Every four years when we sit down to watch the Summer Olympics, we come to that moment when the world turns its attention to races like the 100-meter dash. I remember when Carl Lewis was the fastest human on earth; he could burn up the track. And I would say to my kids, "Kids, can you believe that guy spent *four years* practicing for those *few seconds*?" It got to the point that my kids would mouth the words with me, since I repeated myself sprint after sprint, Olympics after Olympics.

Long races are most graphically illustrated by what many consider to be the most grueling event in the Olympic competition—the marathon. Twenty-six miles of agony. Just the thought of it conjures up pictures of disciplined training. Marathon runners are not known for their speed as much as they are known for their *endurance.* And endurance can only come from a total commitment to the task at hand—being a long-distance runner. Don't get me wrong; sprinters work hard. But their race is over in a matter of seconds, minutes at the most. Long-distance runners train so they can run for hours. All of us want life to last a long time, not just a matter of seconds or minutes. We want our life to last for decades. Therefore, we need to commit to a lifestyle that reflects endurance, a long-haul view. The point is this: it's one thing to run a sprint, but it is quite another to run a marathon.

So, what kind of race are you running in life? If you're running a sprint, then a fast pace and blazing speed are admirable. But if you're running a marathon, running too fast early in the race is disastrous. Your speed will burn you out long before the end of the race.

It doesn't take a rocket scientist to see that the preferred metaphor for life is the marathon. Who would willingly choose a short, fast-paced life?

Imagine going into the downtown of a large city to conduct the typical on-the-street interview. You ask, "What is it you want out of life?" Certainly, a variety of answers would surface, but the gist of all of them would be similar.

"I want to live a long, healthy life."

"I want to enjoy my marriage and my family."

"I want to be successful at my job."

"I want to make enough money to retire well taken care of."

"I want the good life."

However, I doubt you would hear many people say, "I'd like to have it all by age twenty-nine, and then I'd like to drop stone-cold dead right here on the sidewalk. Bury me a contented person!" No, few people with normal intelligence would ask for their life to be characterized as a sprint.

But this is precisely where the metaphor gets tricky. It's been my observation that most Americans try to have it both ways. We try to run life's marathon as if it were a sprint.

It can't be done. Running at a sprintlike pace will drop you out of the long distances. Yet isn't the message we hear in our culture today that the race is won by the swift? This is especially true in business. Sayings like "I need it yesterday!" and "ASAP!" have become clichés due to their overuse. How can we justify that paradox, those opposite extremes?

We can't. This point became abundantly clear to me the day I realized that open-heart surgery, heart bypasses, pacemakers, and zippers in one's chest were no longer the exclusive domain of my father's generation. What was particularly alarming to me was the fact that such medical interventions seemed to speed right by those of us in our forties and fifties, proceeding to young bucks in their midtwenties!

I recall the horror of giving a speech at a corporate event and having a middle manager share with me that he had just returned to work after a quadruple bypass…and he was only twenty-nine! To make matters worse, it was almost as if this were a badge of honor for the guy. It didn't matter to me that his pacemaker was state-of-the-art. I wasn't impressed that it could send faxes, act as a pager, and open his garage door. What was frightening to me was that this guy was so young.

How did it happen? Well, it fit right in with the running motif. This guy was heavily recruited out of business school and chose a firm that would place him on a path for quick promotion. He sped by those of lesser talent and those who refused to sell their souls to the company. He worked long hours like a man possessed. And true to his firm's offer, he was promoted more quickly than any of his peers. What does the corporate world call it when they put a man or woman on this type of plan?

The *fast track*.

It's the track where speed is praised and sought after. The quicker you are, the better. Of course, no one bothers to consider the fact that life's marathon cannot be run as a sprint. So everyone is appropriately surprised when this young fellow is struck down with chest pains or ulcers or any other symptom of a classic case of burnout. And, of course, we'd all be *shocked* if he worked so hard that he actually died!

And that sometimes happens. But business must go on. So after a few days of grieving "this horrible loss," the corporation is accepting applications for a replacement. This new person won't run any slower, either. It's a matter of "chew them up and spit them out, business as usual."

Forgive me if this sounds cynical. I am pleased to tell you that many businesses are waking up to the fact that this travesty is occurring on their watch, and they are making the necessary changes to their thinking. But not all businesses are. As I travel across the United States, speaking in hundreds of business venues, I am consistently taken aside by working men and women who feel trapped by the fast track.

Here's what I tell them:

It is possible to be successful while at the same time maintaining balance between your personal and professional lives.

Life is a marathon, my friend, and the key to any long-distance race is endurance. I hope this book will help more of you reach the finish line so that fewer of you will hit the wall at the 330-yard mark.

Ready? Take your mark. Get set. Let's go.

Two

The Hazies

Why is it so hard to balance work and life? Why do we tend toward imbalance?

Classic illustrations of imbalance abound. Your family is feeling neglected because you haven't been home before nine o'clock one night in the last three weeks. The boss is leaning on you to make that trip to the Canadian client who needs a little extra hand-holding in order to seal the deal. And of course, the dates for the trip conflict with three other work deadlines, not to mention your daughter's piano recital or the concert tickets you've had for months or the getaway weekend you've promised your spouse since the last time you argued about spending too much time at the office.

There are three issues we need to consider: what I call the *Hazies,* the *Lazies,* and the *Crazies.*

Let's look at them one by one.

THE HAZIES

What do I mean by the Hazies?

The Hazies: Losing sight of your long-term goals

Think of haziness, smog, fog.

Of not being able to see what's ahead of you. (I believe it comes from the Greek word *smogos*.) I once heard a highway patrolman point out that when we drive in the fog, we tend to look down. Since we can't see what's ahead of us, we drop our perspective. That's haziness. It's the presence of a fog that keeps us from looking ahead and doing what we should. We know what's important; we just get distracted by something else.

When I was a shot-putter back in high school, I used to love to practice every day in the shot-put circle, right off the track. The location of the circle happened to coincide with the starting point for the one-hundred-yard dash. (This all took place before everything was translated into meters. I know—I am very old.) The race started there so that it would end at the fifty-yard line in front of the home stands. Because of the proximity of the shot-put circle, I was able to overhear the running coach teach his sprinters how to run the race.

"Okay, boys, here's how it works. First, you nail down your starting blocks at the desired location. Then place your feet in the blocks and put your hands along the starting line. Then look up. Find the finish line and focus on the tape. Don't look at anything else until the race is completely over. Don't take your eyes off that tape *until you break it.*"

This coach was way ahead of his time. Long before there were VCRs and videotape, he had found an old black-and-white, sixteen-millimeter movie of one of the first Olympics ever filmed. The movie showed a runner who clearly had a race won. However, just before he finished, he looked over his right shoulder to see how far ahead he was. In that split second, a runner came up from his *left* and beat him to the tape.

It's that kind of distraction that we're trying to avoid in life's race.

If your life's race is like mine, we really don't need another talk, tape, or book on discovering our priorities. We have them written in the front pages of our life notebooks and daily planners. We have them framed on the credenzas in our offices. We have them on our walls, superimposed over breathtaking photos of eagles soaring.

No, we don't need any more material on knowing our priorities.

We need help in *living* our priorities.

We begin our life's race with our priorities and goals in place, but we allow distractions to blur our focus. We start our careers with our hopes and dreams reduced to a series of goals boldly written on a piece of paper. "I will work at this entry level position for a maximum of three years, and then I will move up the ladder in a series of successive promotions until I am in upper management. If this company does not cooperate with my personal plans, I will leave, either to work for a competitor or start my own company." And, of course, life gets in the way pretty quickly, doesn't it? Your mate and eventually your kids *love* where they live, so the thought of moving to the regional office five years later gets put on hold while you try to figure out how to move up the ladder and still keep peace at home.

Just one distraction along the way eventually leads to a series of distractions that sidetrack your career goals in a major way. The same is true in how we begin each workday. We have our to-do list firmly in hand as we seek to live out our priorities and goals. *I need to dedicate the morning to finishing the Rothberg report,* you say to yourself. And your gut, as well as your calendar, agree that this report is an important priority. Then the phone starts ringing. The boss wants you in her office in twenty minutes. Obviously what she wants takes precedence over your plan, but it clearly distracts you from what you intended to accomplish.

And the distractions are usually good things! We want to be good at our vocation. We want to be an excellent spouse. We want to be a great parent. We want to coach Little League. We want to sing in the choir. We want to join the Rotary Club. We want to work out at the health club three times a week. We want to stay current in our reading. We want to be a part of an accountability group. We want to be active in the PTA.

These struggles highlight why maintaining balance is such a difficult task as well as a never-ending one. Many of our goals and priorities end up looking like distractions at different times in our day. So how do we distinguish between the two? In many respects it is like a sliding scale. There are quite a few things that are important to us in life, but which ones are more important than the others?

How you answer this question reflects back to your very core. In the grand scheme of things, what really matters to you? This may take you back to when you first started working or when you first got married or when you started having kids.

How do we do it all?

We've got to stay focused. We've got to avoid the haziness that can distract us.

ARE YOU SUFFERING FROM THE HAZIES?

Are you losing sight of what's important in your life? Most of us constantly struggle to establish and hold to our priorities in our lives. The following checklist may help you discover your level of success over the Hazies. Answer the following questions as honestly as possible.

Do you frequently miss family and personal events due to work-related activities?

Rarely Miss		Miss Some		Miss Most
I	2	3	4	5

Are you feeling less and less connected to the people who are important to you?

Connected		Somewhat Connected		Disconnected
I	2	3	4	5

Do you make time to sit quietly and reflect on the status of your life on a regular, if not daily, basis?

Make Time Regularly		Sporadically		Hardly Ever
1	2	3	4	5

How flexible are you when it comes to scheduling activities? Are you able to "go with the flow," or are you pretty rigid when it comes to your schedule?

Flexible		Somewhat Flexible		Unbending
1	2	3	4	5

Do you drop important tasks for the sake of attending to urgent matters? Focused people accomplish the important things in their day without allowing the urgent ones to take them off track.

Focus on Important		A Mix of Both	Do Urgent, Drop Important	
1	2	3	4	5

How did you score?

5–10	You're doing a good job fighting the Hazies.
11–20	You have good days and bad days; be aware of the Hazies creeping in.
21–25	It's official. You've got a severe case of the Hazies.

THE HARLEY IN THE HOTEL

I've had some great experiences speaking at corporate venues all over the world. I've been in front of some pretty amazing groups, and I've seen my share of unusual presentations. I've been on the program right before former presidents of the United States and right after juggling monkeys. I've set up astronauts and closed for video tributes to wood. But one of the more humorous setups I've seen involved a CEO, a hotel ballroom, and a Harley.

My role was simple: keep the audience awake. After all, this was the dreaded 1:30 slot, right after the pasta-bar lunch. Naps were in order. I was in charge of motivating the crowd with humor, enthusiasm, and high energy.

Right before I was to go on, a handsome, middle-aged man approached me. He extended his hand and introduced himself as the CEO of the company. "Thank you for hiring me!" I immediately responded.

"We're glad to have you," he replied. "I'm speaking right after you. It's the 'State of the Company' presentation."

"I'll do my best to get them pumped up for you," I responded.

"I have a few tricks up my sleeve," he said to me mischievously. "Want to hear about them?"

"Sure. What do you have cookin'?"

He paused for maximum effect. Leaning in, he whispered, "You know, I just turned forty-five."

The counselor in me took over. *Forty-five?* I thought. *He's a classic case of midlife crisis. He's going to tell me about a new girlfriend or a new sports car or a new motorcycle.*

Before I could think any further, he said, "And I just got a new motorcycle."

At least he chose something legal, I thought.

"A brand-new Harley-Davidson," he continued. "Black as night but shiny like the sun."

I smiled, but I had a funny feeling this was going somewhere unusual.

"Anyway," he pressed on, "I'm gonna drive my Harley up onto the stage right before I give my speech." He stopped, allowing the full weight of that statement to sink in. "I've got it all worked out with the hotel. They even built me a ramp. I'll be dressed head to toe in black leather. We're going to pipe Steppenwolf's 'Born To Be Wild' over the loudspeaker system as I ride in. I'm gonna blow everybody away!"

This had the makings of a great speech, so when he asked me if I was planning to stick around, I replied in all honesty, "I wouldn't miss this one for the world."

The time came for my speech. The quiet, sleepy, too-much-pasta crowd came to life as I shared principles on balance in life. When my presentation was over, I walked to the back of the ballroom to see the next part of the afternoon's festivities.

The CEO was in the outside lobby, ready to make his entrance. The music was cued up, ready to rock and roll. It was at this point that it became obvious that my friend, the company president, had neglected to tell me about one important aspect of his presentation. Looking back, I realize the well-meaning gentleman had apparently been to one too many rock concerts. He saw something at one of those arenas that he thought would add to the drama of his entrance.

Smoke machines.

On cue, the smoke machines were triggered. Hindsight tells us now that one smoke machine would have been sufficient in a ballroom of that size. Thus, when the *sixteen* went off, we were in trouble. Simply put, in a matter of seconds you could not see your own hand if it was six inches from your eyes.

Add to this dense fog the soundtrack to *Easy Rider.* For many men and women who were teenagers in the late sixties and early seventies, it was like a bad drug trip revisited.

By the time the CEO got to the stage, people could recognize his voice but couldn't see him at all.

It was a classic illustration of *haziness.* There was the CEO up there. We could hear him, but we couldn't see him. Someone— something—important to every employee's life was blurred by the intense fog in the room. (To be fair to some of my former audiences, I have been in several rooms where the next speaker drove in on a Harley—but only one with sixteen smoke machines.)

There are many important aspects of life, but some of them distract us from the ones that are vitally important. The idea of a smoke machine was fun, creative, and essentially a good thing. But in the end, it distracted us from what was really important—seeing the CEO make his presentation.

Do you know one of the most common illustrations of fog in

our work environment? E-mail. So many good things can be said in praise of e-mail as it relates to saving time, convenience, and efficiency. But check out the average office cubicle. No matter what task is being performed, if we hear the ding alerting us that a new e-mail has arrived, most of us don't have the self-discipline to stay on task. We have to see who it's from, satisfying our curiosity with the justification "It could be something important." What just happened? We got off task by a distraction, a classic wave of fog that kept us from what we really needed to be doing.

Good things can get in the way of better things. If we don't make a mental checklist of what is most important, the vital areas of our lives will get choked out by the thick smoke of life. Maybe one of the items on my mental checklist is that I will check my e-mail only three or four times a day. And to ensure that result, I will mute the volume on my computer, avoiding the temptation that comes with the ding.

It goes back to the race we were talking about earlier. Imagine you are at your home track, preparing to run. You have the roar of the hometown crowd cheering your every move. You have your teammates lined up along the infield, encouraging you as you run. And you have your competitors pushing you to your personal best.

All of these elements are part of the race, and they are all important, but any one of them can cause you to redirect your focus. You need to keep your eye on the tape. Don't take your eye off it until you break it. If you look over to acknowledge the crowd, you're dead. If you turn to make eye contact with your teammates, you've lost. If you look side to side at the competition, you are already defeated.

If we're not careful, we can become distracted and forget what is really important in our lives.

TELL 'EM WHAT THEY'RE DOING RIGHT

Married people or parents will tell you about the importance of their family. But do we live as though our families are important?

I lived in Southern California in the 1980s. It was a time of affluence, greed, and going for the gusto. Every businessperson who was serious about his or her career was reading the same three books. Not only were they read, but they had to be prominently displayed in the office, serving as a badge of business acumen. Do you recall what these books were?

In Search of Excellence

Iacocca

The One Minute Manager

I think back fondly on one of the management gems in *One Minute Manager*—"One Minute Praisings." The concept of "catching your people in the act of doing something right" revolutionized my office staff. I tried praising others one afternoon, and one of my secretaries, motivated like never before, actually began to type. My associates started cranking out work at a feverish pace.

Throughout this book you will see that I have not always been the poster boy for the balanced life. It doesn't take much for me to get off course. This story takes place during one of those seasons of life where I needed a definite course correction. There was a lot going on at work, and I willingly jumped into the pile. No one was holding a gun to my head—I chose to spend more time at the office than necessary. As a consequence, I was not being the kind of parent I knew I could be, simply because I wasn't around my kids as much as I could've been. And when I was home, I was often distracted by thoughts of what I needed to accomplish the next day in the office. You know what I'm talking about—we've all been there.

Driving home that night, I had a flash of insight. "If this stuff works at the office, why wouldn't it work at home?" I decided to tell my kids what they were doing right. Being a father of five, that was no small task, but I was up for it.

When I walked in the front door, I grabbed the first kid I saw. It turned out to be my fourth child and third son, John. He was five years old at the time and a whirlwind of energy.

"Hey, John, come over here. I want to talk to you," I announced.

You know you haven't spent a great deal of time encouraging your son when you invite him over for a chat and he responds, "No, Dad, don't paddle me! I didn't do it, Dad! I think Jeffrey did it!"

Naturally, I was curious about what deed had been done, but I resisted the urge to explore that subject. "Just sit down over here with me, Johnny," I replied soothingly.

"Sit down?" he mused. Sitting down meant giving full protection to the part of his body that would usually receive the paddle. By his smile I could tell things were looking up. But he was still quite nervous. *Stressed* might be a more appropriate word. Have you ever seen a five-year-old stressed? Tiny beads of perspiration rolled off his brow. It looked like a scene out of one of those old black-and-white private-eye movies. All that was missing was the naked light bulb shining in his eyes and an interrogator barking, "Where were you on the night of the fifteenth?"

John took as much of this situation as he could, and then he snapped. He buckled under the weight of the stress he himself had created. He began to confess to all sorts of things he had done wrong over the last few weeks but for which he had never been caught.

I got quite an education. I found myself thinking, *So that's who broke the blue vase. That's who ate my secret stash of sugar cookies. That's where the car was for those three days.*

But all of those issues were off the subject, so I stopped John from his confessions as soon as I could. "We're not here to talk about what you've done wrong," I announced.

"We're not?"

"No."

"Then why are we here?" he asked, genuinely stumped.

"We're here because I want to tell you what you're doing *right*," I replied.

"You do?" he responded in absolute astonishment. "Why?"

"Because I love you, Johnny."

"Oh, I love you too, Dad," he beamed. "So tell me, what do I do that's right?"

And suddenly there was an awkward silence in the room. I immediately realized that I had been so intent on finding each of my five children for this meeting of encouragement that I had neglected to prepare anything to say.

After a moment of reflection, I realized the answer was right in front of me, on top of my little guy's head. At five years old, he was learning how to comb his own hair. Of course, as a typical five-year-old, he only combed the hair that he could see in the mirror—the front two inches of his hair. The rest of his hair was all askew, in the same condition it was when he woke up. But it was all I needed.

"John, John, Johnny." I oozed with delight. "You're learning how to comb your own hair! It looks to me like each day you move that comb a little farther back on your head. Before you know it, you will be all the way back to the crown, and it's all downhill from there!"

John had a grin from ear to ear. "This is great, Dad," he admitted, and then he added, "I love you."

"I love you too, Son." It was a magic moment. Then he asked what my kids always ask me.

"Can I go now, Dad?" Obviously he didn't want the tone of the meeting to change, so he suggested ending it on a high note.

I nodded, giving him a hug and a kiss. In a flash he was gone.

I spent the remainder of the evening hunting down my other four children. By bedtime I had had a meeting with each of them, telling them what they did right.

But as I walked down the hall to enter their bedrooms one by one in order to tuck them in, I discovered all five kids huddled together in one room. They were comparing notes from the evening.

"Did Dad talk to you?" one began.

Another nodded in agreement. "Did Dad talk to you?"

Soon it became apparent to them that I had talked to all of them, and it was all about positive things. This concept was beyond them. They began to panic.

"Is Dad sick?"

"Is Dad gonna die soon?"

"Why would Dad talk to all of us and be so upbeat?"

I smiled, interrupted their meeting, and put them all to bed. As I pondered the evening's events later that night, I was genuinely grateful for having fought through the Hazies in my life that evening in order to live out the priorities I claim.

I learned many years ago that a person on his or her deathbed rarely asks for the laptop or PDA. No, it's the people in someone's life who are of ultimate importance. I want to be surrounded by family and loving friends as life draws to a close, not the latest gadget that will keep me up to date on my financial investments. Yes, one of life's highest priorities is *relationships,* and I unashamedly confess my family is extremely important to me. When they are being neglected, I am not living out my priorities. When I invest in their lives, I am not only bringing them a degree of relational fulfillment, but I am fulfilling a need I have as well.

This story and the ones that precede it illustrate one very important principle: living your life according to your priorities is the best antidote for a bad case of the Hazies. Let's see how we can live out our priorities in practice.

Three

The Priorities Triangle

There is an answer to the maddening question, how can I better balance my work and life? It's understanding and applying your *priorities* in your everyday life. It's been my observation that most of us know our priorities, but few of us put them into practice. Somewhere, someone convinced us that knowing and doing are the same things. They're not. We need to focus on how to move from knowledge to application. Priorities have to be fleshed out in our workaday world in order to have any lasting value.

As I travel around addressing this issue all over North America, I have found that men and women long for a paradigm that will help them achieve greater balance in their lives. Rather than thinking of balance as a tug of war between two issues, each one attempting to pull us off the tightrope, I use the model of a *triangle* to envision a balanced life. It helps make balance more attainable. Three is easier than two. We ride a tricycle before we ride a bicycle, because it's easier. We don't put our expensive camera on a bipod, but rather a tripod, because it lends itself to better balance.

We all know our priorities are important, but how do we achieve those priorities? Let's take a look at the Priorities Triangle:

THE PRIORITIES TRIANGLE©

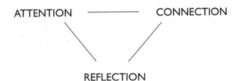

By *attention,* I am referring to the *tasks* we attempt in life. *Connection* speaks to our *relationships. Reflection* has to do with our time of *quiet introspection.* If we can see how these three areas are interconnected, we can move ahead in achieving our priorities.

Organizational psychologists have been telling us for years that people have a tendency to go one of two directions when they manage work tasks. Both approaches get the job done; they just get there from different directions.

Some workers are *task oriented,* meaning that the most important objective in their world is getting the job done. They stick to the task like glue, doing whatever it takes in order to reach a goal. They have used attention as a way to be effective on the job.

Other people are *relationship oriented.* These are the men and women who value their team of co-workers. They use their social skills to understand and relate with the people around them. They get the job done because they inspire those around them to pitch in and do their share.

What we observe on the job we can also see in life. Some of us are more focused on tasks, some of us more on relationships. Neither one is better than the other; it's just the way it is. The key to making the Priorities Triangle work is to ascertain which of these two is your natural tendency and then make a plan that capitalizes on your strength to improve your weakness.

Jack loves people and is a master of networking. He has the fattest Rolodex in town. But Jack doesn't stay on task very well. His love for people distracts his focus on a particular project. "Once I became aware of how my networking was working against me, I decided to take action," he recalls. "I started connecting with people who were more task oriented, and I asked them for help. In a sense, they became mentors to me. Whenever I was tempted to stray from focusing on my task, I called one of my mentors, and he would help me return to what I needed to do. And it worked!"

Rachel needed the opposite help. She was so focused on tasks that she had no social life whatsoever. "The more I thought about my situation, the more I realized I needed help. Being single, I decided that a church singles group was a safe place for me to begin making friends. My first night there I met Jenny, and we immediately began a genuine friendship. We get together every now and then. She helps me move from a task-only orientation to a place where I see the value of relationships. I even volunteered to be a big sister for a struggling third grader. I can use some of my task orientation to guide her in her studies."

What did Jack and Rachel say helped them to understand their orientation? Jack said, "Once I became aware…," and Rachel said,

"The more I thought about it…" They were referring to *reflection,* the third portion of the Priorities Triangle. In order to understand whether you are wired more toward tasks or relationships, you have to sit down and think about it. Reflection is that quiet time of personal introspection when you do nothing but meditate on your life. For years philosophers and religious leaders have known the value of quiet time. But many of us have pushed it aside, seeing it as a luxury reserved for those who have time to waste.

But that's not true. In fact, you can't afford *not* to reflect on your life.

It may be a difficult discipline to begin. Let me share a method that has been helping me for more than twenty years now. I have a little notebook that I carry with me everywhere I go. It is a journal.

I use my journal to record everything about my life. In other words, it is a transcript of all that is important to me. I begin each day by writing a summary of the last day and, more important, how I *feel* about the events of yesterday. It's not enough to say I missed my son's basketball game; I have to describe how it made me feel. Then, as I ponder those feelings, I make decisions for today that will reflect on those issues. If I felt like I cheated my son out of time that he deserves, I won't be talked into another late meeting that will conflict with his schedule. I will come up with a creative way to reschedule the office meeting for the next day. That way I can stay on task and still invest time in my son.

I mentioned earlier in the book about how distracting e-mail can be in our work lives. Research has discovered there is something even more distracting than e-mail. Can you guess what it is? Personal interaction with a co-worker! Obviously we need to connect with our colleagues throughout the day, but I am referring to excessive interaction.

One day I recorded in my journal that I had spent the previous day doing nothing other than carrying on extended conversations with fellow employees. My task-accomplishment total for the previous day was zero—and there was plenty to do! It was during my quiet time of reflection that I realized I needed to be more task oriented before my lack of task productivity caught up with me (that's code for getting fired). Conversely, if my quiet time had uncovered the fact that I hadn't been out of my cubicle since Carter was in the White House, I would have needed to create opportunities to be more social. If nothing else, I could stop eating lunch at my desk and hang out with some co-workers in the lunchroom.

This time of reflection helps me to determine if I am properly balancing my attention (tasks) and connection (relationships). By spending time reflecting on these issues, you can make great strides toward balancing them, thereby allowing you to do the things that are genuinely important to you.

WHAT'S REALLY IMPORTANT?

A few years ago I was invited to address a wonderful group of people in Wichita, Kansas. It was springtime, and the weather was gorgeous. The local flora and fauna were picture perfect, a chamber of commerce dream-come-true. I flew in on a Monday morning and had the entire afternoon to rest at a hotel in preparation for my speech that evening at a local community center.

Around four o'clock I showered and dressed. As is my custom, I turned on the television to keep me company as I got ready. I went for *Headline News* but was shocked to see that all the Wichita stations were overtaken by the Emergency Broadcast System. At first I thought it was a test, but I quickly ascertained that this was the real thing.

A tornado was heading directly toward Wichita. It would most likely hit town about the same time my meeting was to begin. I was stunned. I had gone through hurricanes while living in South Florida and had felt the earth move under my feet during earthquakes in Los Angeles, but I had no experience with tornadoes beyond watching *The Wizard of Oz.* In my mind's eye, all I could see was the community center twirling around and around as I searched frantically for Toto. I was getting nauseated.

So I placed a phone call to my host. "Are you watching TV?" I asked anxiously.

"No," he replied. "Why? What's up?"

"There's a tornado heading straight for us," I babbled. "The local stations have been taken over by the Emergency Broadcast System, saying this is not a test!"

If I'm not mistaken, I heard my host mutter the word *tourist* before he continued. "Bill, everything is just fine. We get these warnings all the time. Don't even give it another thought."

"But we have to cancel the meeting," I blurted out.

"No, we don't. Trust me, the place will be full. Now go ahead and finish getting ready and come down to the community center. Everything is going to be just fine."

When I hung up the phone, I felt like a man sentenced to death by lethal injection. "I'm gonna die," I muttered to myself.

I left the hotel room and slid behind the wheel of my rental car and began driving to the venue. Afraid to be alone with my thoughts, I instinctively turned on the radio for company. Like the television, the radio was filled with more of the same—the Emergency Broadcast System. On every station I tried I heard somber professional voices instructing me on how to prepare for the tornado's imminent arrival. I learned what to do if I was in a house, in a high-rise, in a field, or in a car. The last piece of counsel caught my ear since I was driving at the time. *"If you are in a car, pull over immediately and lie facedown in the nearest ditch!"*

In a panic, I turned my head from side to side, expecting to see car after car veering off the road.

But no one was stopping.

I felt like I was in an episode of *The Twilight Zone*. My instincts were telling me to pull over in an attempt to save my life. But peer pressure was saying, "Stay on the road. Don't be a wuss!"

Plus, I suddenly realized how embarrassed I would be if the tornado didn't hit and I had to show up for my speech all muddy from my ditch experience.

So I bravely drove to town. Just as my host had promised, the venue was full. No one seemed a bit bothered by the potential killer heading our way. I stood up to give my speech and was amazed at how well it went, although I was a nervous wreck. The slightest sound caused me to jump high above the speaker's platform. Thank goodness I jump around a great deal in my normal presentation.

When the meeting was over, I obediently stayed to shake a few hands, but in my mind I was already flying home. I was spooked, and all I wanted to do was wave good-bye to Wichita from the plane.

I packed for the early morning flight home, set the alarm, and went to bed. I was rocked out of a fitful sleep at precisely 1:06 a.m. by the profane ringing of the hotel phone. "Hello?" I muttered, still half-asleep.

"Daddy? Daddy, is that you?"

"Jesse?" I responded to the sound of my nine-year-old son's raspy voice on the other end of the line.

"Oh, Daddy, you're alive, you're alive!" he shouted over the phone. I could tell this was no joke. He meant every word he was saying.

"Of course I'm alive, Son. Why would you think any differently?"

"Daddy, we were just watching the late news here in California. It said a tornado hit Wichita, and I knew that's where you were speaking." He paused, took a long breath, and continued, "The tornado *killed* people, Daddy. I was so afraid that you died. I love you, Daddy. I would really miss you."

The force of this conversation hit me full in the gut. I assured Jesse that I was just fine and that I would be home early the next morning. Once again, he told me that he loved me. I told him that I loved him too, and our phone conversation ended.

But I was to have no sleep the rest of that night. I turned on the TV to see what Jesse already knew. A tornado had struck just north of Wichita, killing dozens of people. I grieved for the families that had lost loved ones, but I couldn't help personalizing what I was watching.

What if it were me? What if I were one of the victims of the tornado's wrath? Am I living my life in a way that would cause me to feel no regrets if death came unexpectedly? These were the types of questions flooding my mind.

There was much about my life that pleased me that night. But there was the continual gnawing sense inside that kept reminding me that the important things in life went beyond dollars and cents, big speeches, and vocational fulfillment.

I was grateful for yet another wake-up call about the importance of keeping balance at the forefront of my thinking.

PRIORITIES EXERCISES

Ask yourself the following questions about each area of the Priorities Triangle.

Attention

What is my mission in life?
Why do I do this kind of work?
Where is my focus these days?
What are my long-term goals?
What are the important things in life to me?

Connection

Who are the three people to whom I am closest?

Are my relationships characterized more by giving or by getting?

Are my relationships characterized by love?

Who would I like to get to know better in the next six months?

To whom am I accountable?

Reflection

Do I set aside a regular time and place for reflection?

What does quietness look like in my life?

What is the most common roadblock that keeps me from a regular time of quietness?

How might keeping a journal help me to achieve more balance?

What qualities would I most like to possess?

Four

The Lazies

The second reason we tend toward imbalance in our lives I call the Lazies.

When I talk about laziness, I do not mean the word as it's traditionally used. I suspect that you and I both suffer from the Lazies, even if we're not lazy in the most common sense of the word. You wouldn't be putting the effort into reading these words if you were that kind of lazy. Here's how I would define the Lazies:

The Lazies: Lacking the self-discipline to bring your life back into balance

It's the ultimate excuse of busy people. "I would change in a minute if I could," they lament. "But you don't understand." And with that they launch into a litany of reasons why "You don't know what it's like…"

...to grow up in a family like mine.

...to have as many financial obligations as I do.

...to have a child with special needs.

...to have the demands I have at my job.

...to have an angry boss.

...to have an abusive parent.

...to grow up poor and now have money.

...to be in this sort of profession/industry/field.

On and on it goes. To these folks, I say two things. First, you're right. I don't know what most of those situations are like—but that really doesn't matter. But second, shifting the focus away from your own responsibility in this matter is keeping you from facing the truth.

It's a common defense mechanism. Therapists call it blame shifting. I can point the finger of blame in a dozen different directions, but ultimately I have to step up to the plate and take responsibility for my life.

ARE YOU SUFFERING FROM THE LAZIES?

As you read my definition of the Lazies, do you find yourself relating in a rather uncomfortable way? Take this little quiz to see if laziness has crept into *your* life.

Is your life currently characterized by balance or imbalance?

Not Balanced		Somewhat Balanced		Balanced
1	2	3	4	5

In general, if something goes wrong, do you take responsibility for your actions, or do you blame someone else?

Blame others		A Bit of Both		Take Responsibility
1	2	3	4	5

Would you characterize yourself as someone who takes time to plan, or do you just go with the flow without much planning?

Go Without Planning		Some Planning		A Careful Planner
1	2	3	4	5

Whether you plan carefully or infrequently, once you've made a plan, how effective are you at carrying it out?

Ineffective		Occasionally Effective		I Work the Plan
1	2	3	4	5

Are you having fun in your life, or is life one tedious task after another?

Boring		Fun Now and Then		A Fun Machine
1	2	3	4	5

So, how did you score?

21–25   You're doing a terrific job of fighting the Lazies!

11–20   You have lazy days and effective days, but you
         can do better.

5–10   Bad news…you are one lazy dude. The good
         news is…*you can fix it!*

LAZINESS IN THE CORPORATE WORLD

The first time I met Charlotte I could tell right away I had touched a nerve with my presentation on balancing one's life. She cornered me after my presentation at a reception that evening in the hotel where the conference was being held. Bright, attractive, full of potential, Charlotte was moving up the corporate ladder the old-fashioned way—she was earning it.

"I just can't find the time to do all that needs to be done in my life," she confessed to me after telling me all the successes in her story-book climb through the stratosphere of corporate America. "I kiss my little ones on the forehead each morning before I begin my day on the job, and I say to myself, 'I will be home to share dinner with them and read them a story before tucking them into bed.' Unfortunately, over the last few months, I haven't made it home before ten o'clock once. My kids are only five and three. They are in bed long before I tiptoe through the door."

As I talked with her about her schedule, she was clear on what had to be done and when—regarding her job. But when I asked her about a schedule with her family, she became painfully vague. "I do what I can to be as available as possible," she stammered. "But you don't understand the demands a job of this nature can put on a person."

I tried to gently suggest she spend some time reflecting on her life in its entirety. "You are more than your job, right?" I asked her.

She nodded, but I could tell she didn't like where she thought this conversation was headed. "Don't ask me to cut back my hours at the office," she said defensively. "I just can't do it and maintain my presence in the company." She glared at me, underscoring the seriousness of her tone. "I've worked too hard to give it all away."

The more I spoke with her that evening, the more I realized Charlotte was *stuck*. There's a real pressure on people in corporate America to work long hours just to maintain their presence in the company. And this is especially true for women in the workplace. What Charlotte needed to understand was that all of us have to make certain sacrifices if we want more balance in our lives. I don't think she was ready to make those sacrifices. But many of us need to do what she was unable to do. We need to become ruthlessly intentional with our schedule. How can I do my required work during office hours so I can spend more time with my family? Are there distractions at work that I can avoid? Is it possible to delegate less-important parts of tasks to associates or subordinates so I'm freed up to do the more important parts? Can I reach some sort of compromise where I work late a few nights each week but make it up with amazing, focused, concentrated family times on the other evenings? The solutions are as numerous as our creativity allows.

Later that evening, in my hotel room, I telephoned my family just to let them know they were on my mind. Charlotte helped me realize how desperately I wanted to achieve balance in my own life.

THE LESSON OF THE NONEMPTY NEST SYNDROME

Do you remember when you were in college, when you were always looking for the easy A? Somebody suggested Psychology 101 or Intro to Family Systems, so you ended up in one of those classes. During the first class period, the eighty-year-old professor placed a pie-chart transparency on the overhead projector. The chart traced the life of a family through its most significant time periods. There was a slice of pie for each of the following stages:

> Newlyweds
> Young Marrieds
> First Child
> The Primary Years
> The Junior Years
> The Teenage Years
> The Empty Nest Years
> The Golden Years

And then you ran out of pie.

Nowadays, when your kids get to college and look for an easy A, those identical classes are still available. As a matter of fact, the one-hundred-year-old professor still puts the pie chart up on the overhead during the first period.

But the pie has changed. There are more pieces of pie dividing up that circle in today's world. Here's my favorite addition. It comes right after the Teenage Years and right before the Empty Nest Years:

The Nonempty Nest Years.

Does that phrase ring a bell with you?

The kid is thirty but still living at home!

There are at least two dozen sociological reasons why the Nonempty Nest Years take place, but here's one of the big ones:

"I'll move out," the son promises his parents, "but not until I can find a place like this one. Or one that's even bigger and better."

This blows his dad's circuits.

"Do you think we started in a house this big?" he asks incredulously. "Ethel, go get the photo albums. Let's show this genius the black-and-white pictures of the two-hundred-square-foot Quonset hut, A-frame, stucco pup tent we lived in when we first got married."

Now the son is incredulous. "You never lived in a house this small!" he cries. "You bought these pictures from the maid!"

What is the point of all this wrangling between the generations? The point is that Junior, even at thirty, lacks a certain character quality necessary to function in a healthy way in the world—patience.

There are plenty of thirty-somethings in the work force who are frustrated with their jobs because they are still at entry level, and it's not exactly what they want. Consequently, they work so hard that they burn themselves out before they even see forty! It is precisely in this sort of situation that patience comes into play. You can get what you're after, but you need to come up with a plan that acknowledges it may take more time than you initially expected. Rather than pushing so hard that you collapse, find things you enjoy about your life right now and relish the moment! "In the zone" doesn't just apply to athletes at the peak of their game. It also relates to all of us who are living our lives at a healthy pace—a pace where we can live out the cliché of smelling the roses. The variety of activities we have in our lives is a wonderful thing.

He is a typical Gen Xer. He lives by the motto "I want it all, and I want it now." But it just doesn't work that way.

There is a wonderful proverb in the Old Testament that says:

As a door turns on its hinges,
So does the lazy man on his bed. (Proverbs 26:14)

Granted, we're not talking about traditional laziness here, but the principle still applies. Most who will read these words are not hinged to the bed. But the question is, if you're not hinged to your bed, to what are you hinged?

- Your job?
- Your golf game?
- Your gourmet cooking class?
- The gym?
- Those people who can advance your career?

Do you see what you're doing? None of those items in the list above are bad things. Just the opposite—they are all good things. But if they become a dominant influence in your life to the point that other parts of your life are being overlooked or crowded out, then you have a problem. By being too firmly hinged to one aspect of your life, you may neglect the other important areas of your life. It's a classic case of imbalance.

WHAT WE COMMUNICATE TO OUR CHILDREN

Whether we fall prey to the Hazies, the Lazies, or, as we shall see later in the book, the Crazies, these tendencies cause us to lose sight of the really important aspects of our lives. Anyone with a family knows the daily struggle of balancing work and home. We love our little kids, but we have a major distraction—our career. There's nothing wrong with career goals. But they, like everything else in life, must be kept in balance.

I remember this event like it was yesterday, even though it occurred many years ago. It was a speaking engagement in a medium-sized city in the Rust Belt region of our country. A picture-postcard-perfect spring day was concluded by a fabulous sunset, which I enjoyed as I drove to the evening meeting in the city's convention center.

The hall was filled with folks eagerly anticipating the evening's festivities. There was a singing group, some drama, a great band, and some wonderful solos. After forty-five minutes of quality programming, it was my turn to go onstage to speak. I had been asked to address the issue of what makes families strong, a personal hot button of mine. Among my points was the issue of spending time together as a family. I related funny anecdotes on this theme as well as sobering stories that brought some of the group to tears.

When I concluded my speech, there was a cordial round of

applause. As the meeting ended, fifteen or twenty people made their way to the front of the auditorium to speak with me about particular aspects of my talk that they appreciated.

I noticed a tall, muscular, young man at the end of the line. He was quite distracting; I kept wondering if he was a professional football player. He certainly had the look of one.

One by one the folks recounted personal stories that related to my speech. About forty-five minutes had passed since the line had formed, but my friend at the end of the line remained faithful. Finally it was his turn. He walked up to me, held out his large hand, and said, "You really got to me with that talk, man." He paused, looking straight into my eyes.

I could tell by looking into his face that he was not joking. His dark eyes welled up with tears, and he took the occasion of shaking my hand to hold on to it, guiding me over to a spot backstage where we could enjoy greater privacy.

"When you told those stories about spending time with your kids, you reminded me of something my son said to me just a couple of weeks ago." Once again he paused, his face tightening with emotion. "You wanna hear what my kid said to me?" he asked.

I swallowed hard and said, "Yes." I knew this would be a difficult moment for both of us.

"My little boy is eight years old," he began softly. "He came up to me the other day right before it was time to put him to bed. I had only been home from work for half an hour. We had been spending very little time together. Anyway, he came up to me and said,

'Daddy, I've been saving all my money!' I thought that was great, so I congratulated him on his accomplishment.

" 'No, you don't understand, Daddy. I've been saving all my money for *weeks and months* now!'

"I let him tell me how excited he was about how faithfully he had put all his pennies, nickels, and dimes into a jar in his bedroom.

" 'Daddy, I've got eight dollars and forty cents!' he bragged. Once again, I complimented him on his frugality.

"My boy went off to his room to play for a little bit, but before long he was back at my feet. He had something on his mind he wanted to clear up.

" 'D'ya know what I really want to do with my eight dollars and forty cents, Daddy?' he asked.

" 'What?' I replied.

" 'I want to give that money to *you*,' he announced.

" 'To me?'

" 'Yes, Daddy, I want to give it to you.'

" 'Why, Son?'

" 'Well, Daddy, if I give you this money, do you think you could stay home from work sometime and play with me?' "

At that point my new friend broke down and began to sob.

"He had me all figured out," he continued once he regained some composure. "Even at eight years old he knew what motivated his father—*money.* He was willing to buy his father's attention…"

And with that he began crying again.

We can blame others all we want, but when the day is done and we look at ourselves in the mirror, we can see who is ultimately responsible for the balance or the imbalance in our lives. If the Lazies are a struggle in your life, you need a good strong dose of endurance. In the next chapter I will tell you how to put it to work in your life.

Five

The Endurance Triangle

Perhaps the Lazies have prospered in our country as a result of our obsession with perfection. We want to do everything we are supposed to in order to have a wonderful life. Years ago my favorite *USA Today* reporter, Karen Peterson, wrote a funny, insightful piece answering the question "How many hours in the day would it take to be perfect?" Tabulating what time experts said we should spend in various weekday activities such as exercise, errands, and time with loved ones, her answers were truly enlightening. It turns out that the perfect day would have to be forty-two hours long in order to accomplish everything!

Karen concludes the article by saying, "Of course, not everyone has children, spouses, pets and plants. And the truly efficient person does several tasks at one time: floss in the shower; pet the dog while making coffee; read the paper pedaling the exercise bike. Another alternative: Crawl into that anxiety closet with your security blanket, suck your thumb, and forget the whole thing."[1]

THE ENDURANCE TRIANGLE©

The antidote to the Lazies is to pursue and practice *endurance*. Remember, life is a marathon; it's a long haul; it's not necessarily about having it all right now. I used to call this antidote *patience,* but I found that word was met with quizzical looks from my audiences. I went home and asked my kids if they knew what *patience* meant and was given this reply by one of my sons:

"Oh sure, I know what it means. Just this morning I was in the doctor's office. The receptionist came out and said, 'The doctor will see you as soon as possible. However, he has nine patients ahead of you.'"

It's not exactly what I had in mind, but it's close.

At a recent meeting where I was speaking, I arrived early enough to hear some of the other speakers making their presentations. One gentleman caught my attention right from the start by speaking on the importance of reducing stress in order to bring peace and longevity to our lives. This presenter was a consummate showman. Throughout his speech, he juggled balls in order to represent all the demands we have in our lives. Starting with three balls, he increased to four, then five, all to the delight of the audience.

"I want you to see how easy it is to juggle," he told the crowd, "so I am going to teach you." The groan in the room was palpable. No one wanted the embarrassment of looking awkward and dropping balls in front of their peers. But the presenter's illustration was pure genius. "This is how we learn to juggle," he instructed. "We don't begin with five balls, nor do we begin with four. We don't even begin with three balls." Things were looking up for the anxious audience. "We don't learn to juggle by juggling balls," he announced. "Juggling is learned by beginning with *handkerchiefs*."

With those instructions, he handed out three handkerchiefs per person. As we threw the cloths in the air, juggling became easy. The pressure of managing all the balls was greatly reduced because the handkerchiefs *slowed things down*. By slowing down, we could do it.

Anything of value in life takes time. So how do we most effectively use the time allotted to us each day? Consider the three aspects of the Endurance Triangle:

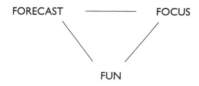

FORECAST ——————— FOCUS

FUN

Forecast speaks to the planning stage of our day. Whether it's early in the morning, at the start of our workday, or late at night in preparation for the next day, planning is an essential part of life. Many of us are wired this way already. We live by a to-do list. There's something wonderfully fulfilling about checking off the items on that list, one by one.

Which brings us to the second part of the Endurance Triangle—*focus*. We have to direct our actions toward working the plan that we put together under the forecast part of our triangle. Not acting on our plan is just as damaging as not planning.

Remember what we learned in the Priorities Triangle? Most of us are instinctively more task- than relationship-oriented, or vice versa. It's important to focus our energies on both areas of our life.

The third portion of the triangle is reserved for *fun*. I include this because, for many of us, it is the most overlooked aspect of our life. We work and work, forgetting how vital it is that we have an opportunity to recharge our batteries. Fun isn't wasted, idle time. Recreation allows us to re-create our energy for the tasks that lie ahead. I will talk about recharging in greater detail later in the book.

Putting this triangle into practice may be more difficult than it appears. Recently I spoke to a major trade association about this topic, and as soon as I was off the stage, I was approached by a young man who introduced himself as Roberto, one of the vice presidents of the association.

"I like what you had to say this morning," he said to me.

"Thank you," I responded.

"I like it, but I have trouble applying it," he continued.

"Give me an example of what you're talking about," I suggested.

"Okay," he replied. "Just last week I got into the office on Thursday a little earlier than I do most days—and I get in earlier than anyone else on my staff—but I knew that on Thursday evening my ten-year-old son had a special event. The idea was to work earlier in the morning in order to put in my full day and then slip out of the office earlier than usual so I could attend his event."

His voice trailed off in a manner that spoke loud and clear that what he had planned didn't happen.

"Everything was running according to schedule," he went on.

"All morning I was getting things done and checking stuff off the to-do list. It was great. And then I came back from lunch. There was a phone message from one of our regional offices indicating there was a minor crisis in the making. I thought half an hour on the phone would be enough to work it through. Three hours later I was still on the call, except now my family was thoroughly disappointed in me."

"So, looking back, what could you have done differently?" I asked.

"That's part of the problem. I don't know! I am a firm believer in planning, or what you call forecasting. But sometimes it's hard to work the plan. Things come up—urgent things—and they have to be dealt with immediately or something terrible is going to happen."

This is as good a place as any to address a difficult issue that many of us must deal with. No matter how we slice it or dice it, there are particularly demanding times in our jobs that will require us to be gone from home more than normal. So how do we handle this potentially damaging situation with our family members?

Ken knows the struggle I'm referring to, and he has also come up with a great solution. "I'm a CPA, and my area of primary focus is tax preparation," he shared with me. "Translated for the layman, that means February through April my life is nonstop. The closer we get to April 15, the less I see of my family. Early in my career I realized it was taking its toll, so I had to scramble to come up with a solution. And actually I think I came up with a good one."

"What did you do?" I asked.

"I made a deal with my wife and kids," he replied. "I started by telling them the truth—you won't see much of me from Super Bowl Sunday until May Day. But…if they could somehow manage without me for that crunch period, I would make it up to them by taking the whole family to Maui for a week in May. It's amazing how well it worked! The older kids helped the younger kids with issues that needed attention from someone with more maturity, and best of all, they weren't seething with anger at me for being gone. Once they understood that there was an occupational hazard to my job, and I admitted it and offered an alternative, they seemed fine. It's not the ideal, but we made the best of what we had."

After I congratulated him on his creativity, he added a sobering caveat. "By the way, since you seem so interested in this idea, I need to tell you that a co-worker of mine offered his family the same deal. But for whatever reason, he never got around to taking them to Maui. He said he was still too busy. It really blew up in his face. His kids are still upset with him."

So for me, the lesson is clear: our families will flex with us when the situation requires flexibility. They'll even help us by picking up some of the slack. But if we make a promise, we better deliver. Kids aren't stupid. If they help us flex and then we blow them off, they won't fall for that ploy a second time. If we try to deceive them, we're toast.

Roberto's plight is a common one. All of us get into these jams, and frankly, some of them are unavoidable. As carefully as we plan, working the plan will sometimes break down. But that shouldn't discourage us from continuing to focus on the Endurance Triangle in order to improve. Balance is far from an exact science, but the more we work on it, the more successful we will be.

I heard from Roberto a short time later. He e-mailed me specifically to let me know life was working better for him once he renewed his commitment to becoming a person of balance!

BOTH/AND OR EITHER/OR

One of the most significant opportunities to come my way early in my speaking career was the invitation to make a presentation to the Young Presidents' Organization. YPO has always been known for attracting the cream of the crop, some of the most successful executives one could ever meet. It was an honor for me to speak at one of their meetings.

As I talked with these folks at the opening reception, I observed the personification of a fairly common maxim: with greater success comes greater responsibility. These men and women were struggling with balance just as we all do—in many cases even more so because of the extra demands placed on them as the CEO of their companies.

Franklin and I hit it off from the start. A handsome young man of thirty-eight, he was as bright as he was good-looking. Running a manufacturing company in the heartland of America provided him with many of life's perks: a house that looked like a seventeenth-century mansion, another home on a lake that looked like a Norman Rockwell painting, top-of-the-line cars, a boat, country club membership, clothes that were tailor-made—never off the rack. And if all of that wasn't enough, God blessed him with a wonderful wife and three of the cutest kids in the world.

Chatting at the reception, Franklin seemed especially interested in my topic. "Balance. Man, you will have a room full of people who need to hear what you have to say on that issue," he mused.

"How about you?" I asked. "Is balance a struggle in your life?"

"No question about it," he replied immediately. "All of us deal with it every day. But there are answers out there if we do the work necessary to find them."

"So what kinds of answers have you found?" I asked, sensing this guy was going to be a wealth of information.

"First of all, planning is essential. It's a cliché, I know, but it's true: if you fail to plan, you'll plan to fail. I believe some of the most valuable time I spend, not only in running my company, but in running my life, is the time I spend quietly planning and reflecting on what my days will look like. In the long run, it will help me avoid potential problem areas in my life."

"Give me an example of a problem area."

"Okay. I know this will surprise you, but some of us CEO types can be guilty of overwork at the office and being a little neglectful of the home front." He smiled ever so slightly to show me he was being facetious. "But a little planning can help overcome that issue," he continued. "Take this past week for example. My ten-year-old had a Little League game on Thursday afternoon. I had a presentation to make for a big client from Dallas on the same day, potentially at the same time. So I got creative. I told the guy from Dallas we were having a baseball theme. He thought I was nuts, but it all worked out.

"I had my meeting after lunch with the Dallas guy. It had originally been scheduled for 4:30, but we moved it up in order to accommodate the 'theme.' At 3:45 we adjourned our meeting, jumped in my car, and drove to the Little League field for the game. My client loved it. He's older, and his kids are grown. He kept telling me how much he was looking forward to this sort of thing with his grandkids. And of course, I scored big points, not only with the client, but more important, with my son. He went four for five that afternoon, including a home run!

"Once the game concluded, I grabbed my son and one of his teammates, and we all went out to dinner. Over the meal, there were times the four of us engaged in conversation that would suit young boys, and at other times the boys talked by themselves, giving me an opportunity for some conversation with my client.

"By the time I dropped my client back at his hotel, he was grateful for the break from the workaday business world. And, of course, when we got home, my son was bragging to the rest of the family about his night on the town with the big guys."

"That's a brilliant idea," I responded.

"You know, we tend to think in terms of either/or. I can either take the meeting with my client, or I can go to my son's baseball game. I prefer the both/and approach. Is there a way I can accomplish both? In this case it worked. I know it won't work in all situations, but that just means I need more time to think in order to plan it out. If I come up with a good plan and work it, the rewards are obvious."

Later that night I was going over my notes for the next day's presentation and couldn't get Franklin's story out of my mind. This guy was actually living out the Endurance Triangle. There was the *forecasting* necessary to envision how the both/and would come to pass. But Franklin did more than think about it. The plan worked because he *focused;* he worked the plan. And it was just too perfect that it surrounded a bit of recreation: hanging out at his son's Little League game—*fun.*

Franklin's story illustrates one of many ways we can creatively incorporate different aspects of our lives into a fun and effective multitasking bonanza! For instance, you could find out if you have clients or customers with interests similar to yours and suggest a meeting that revolves around that interest rather than a boring old meeting in the office! I recently heard of some women who get manicures with business partners instead of a traditional lunch. Maybe you have a client who has the same favorite musician as you, so you could take in a concert together and get a little work done driving to and from the concert hall. The point is, there are myriad ways to mix business with pleasure so you don't miss out on things you want to do—plus you get to build deeper relationships in the process.

The longer I work with these concepts, the more I recognize that the key to this triangle is in the *planning*. Face it, none of this is going to happen if it's not carefully planned out.

Like most of us, I can recall little maxims my grandparents used to set me in the right direction in life. My mother's mother was true to her generation, espousing the value of hard work. *"Don't just sit there; do something!"* she would exhort me, her gnarled index finger pointing at me for added effect. It was wise counsel. Don't just sit around waiting for the world to be handed to you. Go out there and make something happen.

But I am also suggesting there is truth to be found in the opposite of Grandmother's maxim: don't be in a hurry to forecast your future. Take the necessary time to think it through and make the plan both measurable and attainable. And don't forget, careful planning comes from quiet reflection—*don't just do something; sit there!*

ENDURANCE EXERCISES

On the following issues, ask yourself:

- Will the thing that is causing imbalance in my life really matter ten years from now?
- Is it possible for me to do fewer unimportant things at work and outside the office?
- Can I accomplish my goals and be flexible at the same time?
- Can I replace "either/or" with "both/and"?
- Can I work smarter as opposed to harder?
- Can I pencil in time to "Don't just do something; sit there!"?

Ask yourself the following questions, based on the Endurance Triangle.

Forecast

- What issues in life and on the job should I plan for so I can stick to my priorities?
- How can I become more flexible?
- How can planning help me understand what is really important?
- How can I include time-sensitive matters in my planning?
- Do I have a strategy to deal with urgent matters without forgetting about the important things?
- Can planning help me anticipate problems before they arise?

Focus

- How can focusing help me cut down my time spent doing things that don't matter?
- Can I commit to the practice of not adding anything more to my schedule without first taking something else away?
- Can I begin to think in terms of what *must* be done versus what *might* need doing? How good am I at *delegating* tasks or *postponing* them?
- How can I avoid traps like excess paperwork or the interruptions of the phone, fax, or pager?

Fun

- Do I need to plan fun in my life, or does it just happen for me?
- What are the methods I have used in the past for recharging my physical and emotional battery?
- How can I overlap the concept of *fun* with the concept of *connection* from the Priorities Triangle?

Six

The Crazies

There is one other cause for imbalance in our lives: the Crazies. Finally we've reached a word to which we can all relate. It's this state of craziness that probably motivated you to read this book. Here's my definition of craziness as it applies to bringing life back into balance:

The Crazies: Allowing life to run out of control

More and more of us reluctantly identify with this concept. We want to be balanced, but it just doesn't seem to be happening. At work things are in a frantic state on any given day, but the Crazies strike in full force when we agree to "do whatever it takes" to get the project done by its deadline. The result is two weeks on about three hours of sleep each night. Then, of course, we can't understand why we're fighting a lousy flu bug for the next six weeks, including about eight days of sick leave.

Here are some of the common imbalances that occur when the Crazies strike:

- All job, no home
- All kids, no spouse
- All work, no play
- All others, no self

ARE YOU SUFFERING FROM THE CRAZIES?

Are you living a lifestyle that's out of control? Perhaps this checklist will help you gain more insight into your personal level of imbalance. Answer the following questions as honestly as possible.

When was the last time you read a book merely for pleasure?

More Than a Year Ago		Over Six Months Ago	In the Last Thirty Days	
1	2	3	4	5

When was the last time you attended a class or lecture merely for pleasure?

More Than Two Years Ago		Over a Year Ago	Within the Last Year	
1	2	3	4	5

How often do you take time to rest or relax?

Hardly Ever Happens		Sporadically	Make Time Regularly	
1	2	3	4	5

How committed are you to scheduling equal amounts of learning, labor, and leisure?

Uncommitted		Somewhat Committed		Very Committed
I	2	3	4	5

Do you feel as if you have an appropriate amount of control in your job (as opposed to your job running your life)?

No		Somewhat		Yes
I	2	3	4	5

How did you score?

5–10   No question. You've got the Crazies. Read on to learn how to fix them!

11–20   You have good days and bad days. Be aware of Craziness creeping in.

21–25   Nice work! You're either lying, or you're incredibly sane and balanced in your life.

A VERY PERSONAL ISSUE

My personal crucible with the issue of balance came to a boil in 1986. To paraphrase Dickens, it was the best of times and the most unbalanced of times. But looking back, I realize it was absolutely essential for me to experience the feelings I did in order to make the important decisions I had to make.

I was thirty-four years old. It's a good age—you're old enough to finally get some respect from others but still young enough to be filled with idealism and energy. My family was living in Southern California, having relocated there in 1981 from South Florida. We had moved in order for me to take a position as a counselor responsible for helping troubled marriages and treating family crises.

Four years into life as a counselor, I decided to try my hand at writing a book. With a schedule that would make an accountant cheer, I diligently and systematically wrote one chapter a week for fifteen weeks until I had the manuscript finished. It was a book about family life, humorous in approach. After plenty of publishers' rejections and lots of haggling, *Peanut Butter Families Stick Together* was released in 1985. Suddenly I was whisked into the world of book tours, radio and television shows, newspaper interviews, and, most significantly, increased invitations to speak to various groups.

Another element of my vocational life had been a part-time speaking career. I came to California virtually unknown, but through taking any and every opportunity given me, I was now speaking on weekends to businesses, conferences, retreats, churches, PTAs, banquets, bowling alley openings, and bar mitzvahs. It was slow at first, but I gradually built up a fairly regular clientele. With the release of my first book, I became *in demand*. And of course, this pleased me immensely.

Meanwhile, on the home front, things were booming as well. In August 1985, our fifth child was born. We had a daughter and four sons, ages nine, eight, five, three, and newborn. Five kids kept us plenty busy.

Anybody with lots of children can see where this story is

headed. Everything was happening at once. Five vibrant, healthy children want time with their dad. There's nothing wrong with that, right? And a loving wife deserves time and attention as well. It would make sense to anybody.

My career was really starting to take off. The book was selling, and I was being invited to speak at places to which I had always hoped to be invited. It was a time I look back on as personally fulfilling. I was providing education and encouragement to people all over the country. It felt good, like a calling. Yes, that was it—a calling to strengthen and encourage people all over the United States. I liked the way that sounded as it rolled off my tongue.

And, of course, the clincher to the whole deal was the money. I was being paid a good salary as a counselor. Add on top of that honorarium checks for speaking, royalty checks for writing, and checks from the sales of audio- and videotapes, and you've got an enticing financial equation.

By mid-1986 I was awaiting the release of my second book, *My Kids Are My Best Teachers,* accepting invitations from all over the United States and Canada, and still counseling Monday through Friday in Southern California. I was on top of my world, I thought. I perused my calendar and discovered I was booked for *thirty-eight* of the year's fifty-two weekends! Reading that figure now, you might wonder why I didn't know enough to pull in the reins. But as many of us have experienced, success is intoxicating. It's difficult to pull away from the table when the banquet is so sweet.

A typical week found me working nine- or ten-hour days during the week, except for Friday. That day, I took off early and caught a bus that took me from its origination point at Disneyland down a maze of freeways to Los Angeles International Airport. I flew somewhere, spoke Friday evening, all day Saturday, and Sunday morning. Late Sunday afternoon or early that evening I boarded another jet for the flight home. After coming back on the bus from LAX to the Magic Kingdom, I then found my little Honda parked at the Disneyland Hotel and drove home late Sunday evening.

Most weekends the kids were already asleep before I returned. I remember the guilt I felt at not being able to see my children awake. But when you're on the fast track, you learn to stuff that guilt back down, along with a mixture of other emotions that would keep a therapist busy with you for years. To further complicate matters, as well as proving my power over my guilt, I usually rose early Monday morning in order to get to work before anyone else. That way I could make up the work I missed by leaving early on Friday afternoon.

The result of all this busyness was that I often went days at a time without seeing my kids. When I helped tuck them in on Thursday evening, it could be the last I would see them until our evening meal on Monday. But it never struck me as imbalance. "This is how all my friends live," I rationalized to my wife, my friends, and myself.

Following the normal patterns of child growth and development, our newborn, Joseph, took off in the world of infants. He learned to crawl; he learned to walk; he just seemed a little slow in the talking department. His sister, Joy, and his brothers, Jesse, Jeffrey, and John, were all talking by the time they reached his age. But all kids begin talking on their own schedule. Whereas the other four had "goo-gooed" for months, leading up to the use of actual speech, Joseph marched to his own drummer. It was as if a switch went off in his brain one particular day. He awoke in his crib, his first thought being, *Today is the day I will begin to talk!*

I'll never forget it as long as I live. It was a Monday evening dinner. I had been on one of my weekend junkets to who knows where, and I was looking forward to seeing the kids and being updated on all that was going on in their lives. We all gathered at the dinner table in our regular places. Joseph was in his high chair, between his mother and me.

Remembering that today was the day to speak, Joseph chose that moment at the dinner table to enter the world of speech. In a rare slice of silence, he turned to his mother and said with crystal clarity, "Hey, Ma!"

Before we could rejoice over this major accomplishment, he turned to me and said, "Hey, Bob!"

I felt like I had been struck by a stun gun. My son had spoken, but what did he say? "Hey, *Bob*"?

His mom and I looked at each other blankly. She broke the silence by saying, somewhat facetiously, "You've been on the road too much!"

Returning sarcasm for sarcasm, I retorted, "Never mind that. Who's Bob?"

Dinner proceeded as usual, and I listened as my children filled me in on the events of their lives that I had missed because I was "so successful" at my job. After the meal and after the dishes were cleared and cleaned, I talked with my wife about my uneasiness.

"He called me Bob," I mumbled.

"Oh, relax," she replied. "It was an innocent thing. He doesn't think you're Bob. You're his daddy."

"But that's just the point," I countered. "I've been so busy working a forty-five- or fifty-hour week, plus all these weekend trips I'm making, that he doesn't have any reason to know I am his daddy!"

She sat quietly and allowed me to continue.

"I'm thinking of starting a club," I rambled in a mixture of anger and sadness. "I'm going to call it the Flashlight Fathers. It's for all those dads like me who leave for work so early each morning and come home from work so late at night that they never see their children awake. Their only contact is when they sneak into their kids' room and shine a flashlight on their faces. Once they see the normal breathing pattern, they convince themselves that everything is all right, and they're off to their work."

Once again there was silence.

"It's a very prestigious group, the Flashlight Fathers," I went on. "Do you know why? Because we are all very successful, not only at our jobs, but also in our parenting."

More silence.

"Think about it," I explained. "I never feel more successful as a parent than I do when I watch my child sleep! The kid doesn't mouth off, doesn't disobey, doesn't show disrespect. He just lies there and breathes, the way most of us think it was intended.

"Maybe it's time to rethink what I'm doing with my life," I concluded.

And that is precisely what I did.

That night was an epiphany for me. I was so caught up in helping everybody else in the world, I thoughtlessly neglected my own family. To this day, I am so grateful to my wife and kids for hanging in there with me during that difficult time and holding everything together.

THE EPIDEMIC KNOWN AS "THE CRAZIES"

When I reflect on that time in my life, I see that I was suffering from a malady that is sweeping our culture—the Crazies, *a lifestyle that is out of control.*

"You just don't understand all the demands that are being placed on me right now" is the anthem of the crazy. "I'm under so much pressure at work right now. I've got to produce this report for our client by the end of the week. It's one of the most important presentations I'll make, because there is currently an opening for a better position in the company. I truly believe if I do a good job on this account, I will be offered this promotion. It's what I've been working for over the last seven years.

"I know I'm missing Little League games and choir concerts and piano recitals and Christmas pageants, but, hey, there's a lot of financial pressure resting squarely on these two shoulders. Time for those things will come. Believe me, my goal is to get to the point where I can make time for those sorts of things."

It's a time of tremendous ambivalence. The people who suffer from the Crazies go to bed each night feeling successful yet overwhelmed by the loss in their life. The nagging feeling that consummating the deal should have felt better haunts them. The promotion should be more exhilarating. The acquisition should be more satisfying.

But it's that face encircled by the beam of a flashlight that cannot be erased from their memory. It's the realization that too much of his or her little life is speeding by. They're missing out on what's really important, choosing instead to bask in the accolades of the corporate climate—those who approve, endorse, and even encourage such behavior.

That's the sort of feeling Pete wrestles with. I first became acquainted with Pete when I spoke for the company that employs him. It's a Fortune 500 company with a name everyone would recognize. After my speech, he asked me if I could have a cup of coffee with him in the hotel's coffee shop. I had some free time and agreed.

"Your presentation on balance was really right-on," he began.

"Thanks, Pete. I appreciate the kind words."

"Yeah, actually, I'm kinda surprised that this company would allow you to give that kind of presentation to its employees."

"Is that so?"

"Let's just say no one who works here would ever say this company is promoting a balanced lifestyle. Frankly, it's just the opposite. I am under constant pressure to work long hours. It's pressure from above on the organizational chart, and then it becomes peer pressure. Everyone feels like this is what you *have* to do in order to succeed. We make one impossible deadline, in complete exhaustion, only to have another one, equally as unrealistic, immediately thrown on us. And there is an unstated message that if you don't comply, you'll be out the door at the company's earliest convenience.

"I am riddled with guilt. I go home to a wife who is angry, kids who feel ignored, and a house full of fix-it jobs that have remained unfixed since we moved in five years ago. I feel stuck."

"Well, Pete," I said, "from where I'm sitting, I see three possible options. Number one, you can leave things the way they are and, in doing so, slowly but steadily destroy yourself and your family. I call that option 'Feeling the Heat.' The second option is to cut back on your time at work. The third option is to quit and seek work elsewhere. Those last two options I call 'Seeing the Light.'"

Pete sat stone faced for a minute. "Well, I sure don't want things to stay the way they are. That's just not an option."

"Then we've narrowed it down to two."

"But I can't cut back my hours. You don't understand this particular corporate climate. It would never fly."

"Then I guess you'll have to quit."

"I can't quit."

"Then you'll have to cut back your hours."

"I can't cut back my hours."

"Then you'll have to quit."

"I can't."

"So let's go back to option one and keep everything just the way it is."

"Gee, Bill, you're not budging much on this issue, are you?"

"I don't see how I can budge and still help you. I don't mean to oversimplify, but it really does boil down to one of those three options."

The cup of coffee ended without our resolving Pete's dilemma. But we agreed to stay in touch by phone and letter. Six months later I received a phone call from Pete that brought resolution.

"Hi, Bill. I wanted you to be one of the first to know that I made some big decisions in the last month. I went home after our conversation at the hotel and talked long and hard with my wife. We agreed that something needed to be done. I checked into the possibility of cutting back, and just as I suspected, it really didn't pan out. So I began a quiet but intensive search for similar work for another company that would be more understanding of my need for balance. To my amazement, there was a company that understood, had a position open, and was willing to hire me!"

"That's great, Pete!" I exclaimed.

"A week ago today I resigned. The boss was shocked. He gave me a long spiel about throwing away a golden opportunity, but I told him I was clear in my conscience concerning my decision."

"I'm proud of you, buddy!" I rejoiced.

"Thanks, but it's going to be a little rough for a while. The truth is, I took a substantial cut in pay, and I'm coming into this new company at a much lower level. But, as my wife and I discussed the whole issue, we felt we could make it on the money I will be paid, and the cutbacks we will need to make will probably be good for us anyway."

"It sounds like you have really thought this through," I said.

"I have. But you know what confirmed the whole thing? I went into my ten-year-old daughter's room and told her about my decision. I shared with her how sorry I was for missing out on so much of her life so far and that my intent was to be around a lot more as a result of this new job. Well, she broke down and cried. I thought she was sad, but she kept saying, 'Daddy, I am crying because I am so happy. I have missed you so much. I can't wait to spend more time with you.'" He stopped abruptly. It was obvious he was choked up after relaying his daughter's message.

We rejoiced a little more and then concluded our call. Faced with an incredibly tough decision, Pete made it work.

However, if you are overworked, it doesn't always require a resignation. Ellen had a situation arise with her kids where she needed to come into work later a couple of days a week and to leave early on Thursdays. Once she convinced her boss that, even with these concessions, she could still get in the number of hours required to do her job, they incorporated a flextime policy at her job. Granted, it took an understanding boss, but your boss may be nicer than you think!

THE CRAZIES: AN EQUAL OPPORTUNITY EMPLOYER

Cases of the Crazies are not limited to those who respond to the crack of the corporate whip. Out-of-control lifestyles can be seen across the board, no matter what kind of job you do or the size of your company. It can affect everybody at some time or other: from hard-driving Type A's to meek and quiet people helpers. And it's not just in the "for profit," bottom-line-driven world. Craziness knows the world of the nonprofit as well.

Kevin is a pastor in America's heartland, the Midwest. His congregation is one that church-growth experts would call small to medium in size. Kevin has the help of only two other full-time staff pastors, which translates into lots of late nights and early mornings for Kevin.

"When you're in the business of ministering to people, you can't expect them to drop everything for you," Kevin explained to me one morning over a cup of coffee. "It's actually just the opposite; *you* have to be available to them."

"So what does a typical day look like for you?" I asked.

His bushy blond eyebrows rose as his forehead furrowed. "Well, that's part of the problem, Bill," Kevin responded. "No two days are alike. There are certain things you can count on—church staff meeting every Tuesday at 10:00, elder meetings every other Monday evening at 7:30, and, of course, the Sunday services. But that's often where the predictability ends."

"Tell me what you mean," I urged.

"I have a list of people whom I need to meet with one-on-one. In order to comply with their schedules, I have to be willing to do breakfasts at 5:30 or after-dinner sessions that can often eat up an entire evening."

"Is that a regular issue?"

"Yeah, I would estimate that I do about four breakfast meetings a week, plus five evening commitments. And this is all besides Sunday."

"Tough schedule for a guy who's trying to raise a family," I mused.

"Tell me about it! I haven't even mentioned the last-minute pressure to produce a sermon each week that is of the caliber of these guys you hear preaching on the radio every day. It's an unusual Saturday night when I'm in bed before 2:00 a.m. Then I'm up at 6:00 to put the polish on it one last time. It gets old, believe me.

"Regina is always getting on me that I don't spend enough time with our kids—and she's right. Last Saturday I blew into Glen's Little League game at the end of the fifth inning. He had already played and was sitting on the bench. Then I find out he had hit a ball that almost went over the fence! His first triple, and I'm off with some volunteer committee! It's getting to the point that I'm hoping he won't play or else won't have a good game until I get there! How selfish can a guy be?"

Much of what is developed in this chapter was presented to Kevin over the weeks that followed this conversation, and it made a difference in the way he went about his life's race. In short, Kevin didn't feel the need to resign his pastorate, but he did exercise some intentional creativity in adjusting the amount of hours he put into his work.

One element Kevin learned that is helpful to all of us is learning to say no. Granted, we are not all in a position to decline certain things that come our way, but you'd be surprised how much control you do have in your life. If your boss tells you to do something, I suggest the best answer is yes. But I am referring to the countless other demands we have in life that we say yes to. Perhaps it is not a good time to take on a few more customers. Maybe this is a bad time to volunteer for one more committee. If not "no," at least consider "not right now." That one works too.

Kevin is living a more balanced life these days. Regina feels like she is married to a new man, and the kids are going around school bragging that they got "a new daddy" (causing the need for some explanation to the adults in his congregation!).

My Personal Race Minus the Crazies

When my child called me by another person's name, I knew something had to be done. For many months I had been feeling the heat, and I knew it was time to see the light. From that point on, changes were made—big changes. It took some time to bring them to culmination, but that night I realized I could no longer work at all my endeavors.

Conventional wisdom said to do away with the speaking and concentrate on my job as a counselor. But the process was complicated by the fact that I greatly preferred the weekend speaking to the weekday counseling. I felt a greater use of my gifts on Saturday and Sunday.

Where do a person's gifts come into play? Are we sentenced to merely going through the motions in a job that is less fulfilling than that which we'd really like to do? Is it a pipe dream to think that we can truly do what we want to do in this world? Can we actually do what we love and have the money follow?

This was not a decision I felt comfortable making alone, so I invited five other couples into our home one evening for the express purpose of answering the question "What should I do with my life?"

"There's no question you're a gifted speaker, Bill," a close friend began. "I think you would be very successful on the speaking circuit."

"By not working your counseling job, you would free yourself up for more time with your family," his wife added.

"It would be a sort of 'feast or famine' thing," another chimed in. "It sounds like when you'd be working, you'd be out of town, only able to communicate with your family by phone. But when you're home, you'd be home completely. No office to go to, no staff to manage, no time clock to punch."

"Sounds pretty good to me," my best friend said, smiling broadly.

Everyone was nodding in agreement, their faces filled with the radiant joy of giving birth to a new dimension in a man's life.

Everyone was smiling…except me.

"Is something wrong, Bill?" my best friend asked.

I swallowed hard. This was so ironic. Here I sat encircled by my best friends as they promised their love, encouragement, and support to help launch me in a career direction that made the most sense of any option I had ever heard. Yet my stomach was churning inside as if I had just downed eight burritos with extra salsa. There was a sharp pain behind my eyeballs. My mouth was dry, and my hands were moist. I searched for the right words to explain the emotions I was experiencing at the time. Finally the words I needed came to mind.

"I'm scared," I volunteered meekly. "You all are being so supportive, it's overwhelming. I know I have the best friends in the world, based on what I have heard here tonight. And your level of confidence in my ability is truly humbling." I paused and took a deep breath, trying my best not to hyperventilate. "I just wish I had the same confidence you do. I'm responsible to care for and feed this wonderful family I've been given. Failing at that privilege would be the most horrible failure I can think of. I'm frightened."

At that point our business meeting turned into a soul-searching experience. One by one, all of these dear friends comforted me, encouraged me, and prayed for me. We put a plan in motion that included reestablishing contact with my former speaking clients, informing them of my new availability, together laying out a business plan on paper, resigning my counseling position, and aggressively going after as many speaking assignments as I could manage. With my new full-time job being "speaker and writer," I could book more gigs without feeling as though it was pulling me away from home on nights and weekends. It was now my career!

Moving on from the counseling position was frightening, but it was also freeing and energizing. So much of the launching process goes back to that evening when a frightened thirty-four-year-old took a big step toward the strength, courage, and peace he needed to move into a new venture.

Henry knows the value of trusted friends. A hard-charging CEO of a manufacturing company, he shared with me how he had developed a condition he referred to as "executive blinders." He couldn't see the full picture of what was going on in his company. In order to gain some perspective, he turned to a small group of friends who were able to open his eyes to his blind spots. In doing so, not only did they save the company a lot of money, but they saved Henry from a huge amount of grief and stress.

How can you overcome the imbalance created by the Crazies?

It's time for the runner's equivalent of balance: pacing.

Seven

The Pacing Triangle

S o how are you going to beat the Crazies? There is a way, and it is the key concept in this little book. If you master this one, you're well on your way to achieving a successful and balanced life.

It goes back to the metaphor of life as a race. We can't run a marathon like it's a sprint! Several years ago I was attracted to the cover story of a *Runner's World* magazine. The article was entitled "The Perfect Pace," and in it Amby Burfoot and Bill Billing Jr. discussed the importance of pacing in a runner's success.

> For too many years runners have been told to train as they feel. The problem is that no one tells you how you're supposed to feel when you're training right. Lacking this, many runners unconsciously fall into the "no pain, no gain" trap. They train too hard. You know what comes next: burnout, fatigue, injury.
>
> Without any other guidelines, [runners will] no doubt continue training the same way.

Ask yourself the following question: At what pace should I be training to maximize my fitness and my racing performances? If you can answer this question, you have the key to a successful training program.

But we're betting you can't answer it. We doubt you know your optimal training pace.[2]

Were these guys writing about running, or were they writing about life? I think the answer is a resounding "Yes!" on both counts. What happens when you run life's race at the "no pain, no gain" pace? Burnout, fatigue, and injury. Frantic running leads to a fractured life.

The Pacing Triangle©

To beat the Crazies, you must pursue and practice *pacing*. If you're going to make it as a long-distance runner, you must pace yourself. If you run like the wind for the first half of your race, there's a chance you will run out of steam before the full race is over (remember my 330?).

Here's what the Pacing Triangle looks like:

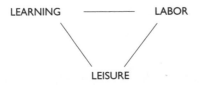

THE THREE BOXES OF LIFE

The inspiration for the Pacing Triangle is an old book by Richard Bolles entitled *The Three Boxes of Life and How to Get Out of Them.* In that book the author presents three aspects of all lives: *learning, work, and play,* which I have renamed *learning, labor,* and *leisure.*[3] With sincere gratitude to Mr. Bolles for the premise of this idea, allow me to flesh it out further.

As soon as children are born in this country, they are thrown into the box of *learning.* This is the box that says, "Let's get this kid into a good preschool, so we can get him into a good elementary school, so we can get him into a good high school, so we can get him into a good university, so we can get him into a good graduate program, so we can get him into a good postgraduate program!"

If your kids are like my kids, somewhere in this process (usually sooner rather than later), they ask the inevitable question, "Why do I have to go through so much schooling?" And what is the answer all parents have been taught as a response? "You have to go to school so you can get a good job!"

That comment catapults our child from the first box to the second one—the box of *labor.* Most likely, this is the box you are in right now. It's the box of work, the box of the job, the box of making a living. You work, work, work. Vacations? Only for the wimpy. Further your education? Only if it will provide you with a promotion—at work!

This monotonous vocational routine goes on and on. Eventually someone, like your spouse, will raise the question "Why are you working so hard?" What is the answer we all know so well? "I'm working this hard so that one day I can retire!"

The banquet is lavish, the speeches are complimentary, the gold watch is bestowed, and you are now in the land of the AARP. And that's our third box, the box of *leisure*. It's the box that says, "I'm finished working, so I'm going to buy me a condo on the fifth fairway of the golf course. I'm going to play 135 holes a day, and when I die, they will cremate me and spread my ashes all over the thirteenth green. Since I could never par that hole, I'll kill it!"

Now, there is a fourth box they will put you in, but rather than be morbid, I'll leave that one to the mortician.

The contrast to living in the three boxes of life one at a time is constantly *moving through* the three boxes in each stage of life. I call it *leapfrogging*. Let me explain.

For our children or grandchildren in the first box of life *(learning)*, it is important for us to help them move through the other two boxes as well. Learning is the law. If the kid doesn't go to school, the parent goes to jail, so we have one box covered. And kids love to play. They'll do so on their own with little or no help from us. Where children need help is with the box of *labor*. One of the best gifts we can give our children is to teach them the value of work. How? Get them working as early as possible. Give them chores to do at home. Or better yet, get them their first job the same way you got yours— lie about their age! Okay, we don't want to teach dishonesty, but we will give our sons and daughters an advantage above their peers if they learn to embrace work the way they do learning and leisure.

What about those of us in the work force box of *labor*? We need to become intentional at getting involved in the other two boxes. All work and no play make Johnny a dull boy. So we have to get creative. For example, if we're talking about the box of *learning,* when is the last time you read a book? I'm not looking for a work-related answer. If you're in accounting, the answer should not be, "I just finished reading the updated United States Internal Revenue Code." When was the last time you read something for the sheer enjoyment and educational value it brought you? I ask this question in my presentations to corporate groups. The most common answer I am given is this: "The last book I read just for the fun of it? It would have to be back in eighth grade—*Little Women*!" So take a lesson from my corporate friends and don't be afraid to do a little reading on the side just for the fun of it.

And speaking of learning for fun, why not consider going back to school? Before you get all stressed out about an MBA program or a PhD dissertation or whatever, let me explain the kind of "going back to school" I am talking about. Have you considered taking night classes or weekend classes simply for personal enrichment? Okay, maybe you can't bring yourself to take French Literature of the Fourteenth Century or Art Appreciation of the Ming Dynasty. But you could do it if you wanted to.

Even if you feel you must take a computer class or a finance course, there is a stress-free way to do it. Having taught at the college level for well over a decade, I will gladly let you in on a great academic secret—*auditing a class.*

It's not like an IRS audit; it's just the opposite. IRS audits create stress. Auditing a class eliminates stress. By auditing a class, you are not taking the class for college credit. Unless you are convinced that you will need this class for your MBA or PhD, you can enjoy some definite advantages. For one, you pay a reduced rate, since you won't be receiving any credit.

Here are the other advantages. When I audit a class, I usually go up to the professor during the first break of the first class and introduce myself with the following little speech: "Hi, I'm Bill, and I just wanted you to know how much I am looking forward to your class this semester. Oh, and by the way, I should probably tell you that I am auditing your class. So, as I understand it, that means I don't need to read any of the assigned readings or complete any of the term papers or take any of the tests. I guess it means I don't even need to show up for class if I don't want to! Well, anyway, thanks for all your hard work. I know it's going to be a wonderful course!"

The professor is usually furious. But what's he going to do, fail me? He can't. I've already flunked! Technically, by not taking the course for credit, I have no grade anyway. So go ahead; take some classes for fun.

And then there is the box of *leisure.* Are you having any fun while you reside primarily in the working box? I can just hear your answer: "A little vacation here, a long weekend there, a few hours of fun at a work-related conference." But I mean a more serious view of fun. I want you to become more intentional about scheduling times of rest, relaxation, and personal enjoyment. Why? It recharges your physical, mental, and emotional batteries.

As a personal example, I used to go to great lengths to hide the fact that I enjoy playing golf. I went through a stage when I played golf only in conjunction with a business trip—meaning I never played golf in my hometown. How could I justify four or five hours out on the golf course when I could be using those four or five hours to advance my career? A valid question. The truth is, you probably could do something more productive with your leisure hours. But if you don't take some time for fun, who knows what shape you'll be in when you're finally able to retire? No one wants to dwell on his demise. But face it; if you don't take care of yourself, you may very well cut your life short, and all that extra work on the career will have been in vain.

So whether it's golf or tennis or jogging or the local bowling league, make sure you have some *leisure* planned into your workaday world.

I'm pushing these points pretty hard because I believe it is important to have learning and leisure in your life that are unrelated to business. However, having said all that, it is certainly acceptable and in some cases helpful to combine learning and leisure in a way that helps you on the job. Reading books in your field of endeavor can only help you improve as an effective worker, so I would never discourage you from that practice. Just remember to read outside your field as well.

Same goes for leisure. I speak at many corporate functions that are off site, specifically built around a fun venue. The company does this as a reward for a good year or good quarter or the achievement of some goal. You can have fun while working; just make sure you have fun outside of work also.

For those of us who are in the box of *leisure,* remember that *learning* and *labor* are still important as well. Retirement is great, but a permanent state of stagnancy is not. One of the finest examples I know was the retirement phase in the life of my father. Bill Butterworth Sr. worked all his adult life for the Reading Railroad in Philadelphia. He retired in his sixties with forty-one years of service. A few weeks after his retirement I received the following phone call. I was home in Southern California, and my dad was home in Philadelphia.

"Dad, how are you doing?" I asked.

"Okay," he replied weakly. "Well, not really," he added.

"What's wrong?" I inquired.

"Well," he stammered, "it's your mother. (long pause) She's driving me crazy! (another long pause) But don't worry, I just took care of it."

There was something in the way he said that last statement that had my mind conjuring up pictures of my mother lying dead on the carpet in front of the couch.

"What did you do, Dad?" I blurted.

"I just got me a job!" he proudly announced.

"You did what?" I exclaimed.

"Don't worry, Son. It's part time, so it won't affect my Social Security," was the answer he thought I wanted to hear.

"What kind of job did you get?"

As only a senior could answer, he replied, "I got a job down at the old folks' home. I take old people to their medical appointments at the local hospital. They've given me a brand-new fifteen-passenger van. I drive three days a week, and most days the van is full."

He continued to regale me with stories of how he would be not only their driver but also the floor show. "I give 'em my best jokes. They laugh like crazy. I'm really working on my bit!"

It was while he was telling me this same story over and over that he finally let slip a key detail. "Yeah, the fifteen-passenger van is usually full, and some days there are three people with medical appointments!"

"Whoa, Dad. Did I just hear you correctly? Did you say you drive fifteen people to the hospital and only *three* of them have appointments?"

His reply? "Have you ever been in one of those old folks' homes? It's pretty boring in there. There's nothing to do. All the action is on the way to the hospital. The van is where it's at!"

Well, I don't know if I agree with my father's assessment of "old folks' homes," but I do have to admit that he had a good handle on the advantage of lifelong labor. And when it comes to lifelong learning, I will never forget the hours he spent helping children learn to read, even while he was still working on the railroad. His tutoring sessions were as beneficial to him as they were to the darling elementary students he taught.

Lifelong learning, lifelong labor, lifelong leisure. That's the Pacing Triangle. It's a proven strategy for a successful life. Make it yours.

PACING EXERCISES

1. Divide your life's race into *laps*. A lap is any person, place, or thing that puts a demand on your time. Here are some examples:

- Your spouse
- Your children (Remember each child is an individual lap. In my case Joy is a lap, Jesse is a lap, Jeffrey is a lap, John is a lap, and Joseph is a lap. Total: five laps.)
- Your job (If you have more than one, count them all. In my life, for example, *writing* is one lap, and *speaking* is another. Total: two laps. For some, your job will be a long list of laps—and that's okay. A friend of mine has his vocational life divided into *eight laps*! Remember, I would much rather have you overdo this exercise than underplay it. The key is to create an accurate representation of your life right now.)
- Your leisure (golf, tennis, boating, reading, relaxing, etc.)
- Coaching Little League
- Church or synagogue
- Accountability group
- Working out three times a week
- The office bowling league
- Reflective time alone

2. As you look at your laps, can you prioritize them? Instead of just numbering them, try this technique. Give the most important laps in your life an A, the next level of importance a B, and those that are comparatively unimportant a C.

3. As you review the laps that make up your life, would you conclude you have…

- Too many?
- Too few?
- Just right?

4. Where do you tend to concentrate?
5. What tends to get overlooked? (In answering numbers 3 and 4, consider both *time* and *attitude*.)
6. What coincides with your priorities?
7. Why is this particular lap important? (For you personally, or to please someone else?)
8. Should you talk this over with your partner? (Best answer: yes.)
9. Should you talk this over with someone to whom you are accountable? (Best answer: yes.)

Now think about the following questions that come from the Pacing Triangle.

Learning

What class would be enjoyable and enriching for you to take?

What is the last book you read, and when did you read it?

What book would you enjoy reading?

What is the biggest hurdle to overcome regarding learning? How can you get over it?

What form of learning do you only dream about? How can you make that dream a reality?

Labor

How can you be more efficient at work?

What would make your work more significant?

How can you refocus your job so that it helps you achieve your life's goals?

How do you prioritize?

How can you learn to focus on the most important clients and customers you have, while still getting all your work done?

Leisure

What is your favorite form of leisure?

How can you incorporate it into your routine?

How can your "fun" activities even benefit you at work?

Are you getting enough exercise?

Are you eating healthy?

Are you getting enough sleep?

How can you better mix business and pleasure?

Eight

Moment by Moment, Day by Day, Year by Year

Balance. It's one of those issues that demands constant attention. You don't nail it all down in one shot; you must come back to it again and again. I know whereof I speak. I have struggled with balance my entire life, and still it needs my constant attention.

My five children are grown now, but I am thankful for all the lessons they taught me about what is really important in life. More than twenty years ago I was taught an insight by my oldest son that I have never forgotten. I think it serves as a fitting conclusion to the points I've been discussing. I described it in my journal in 1983, the year it happened. It is as fresh today as it was back then:

There's something magical about a birthday when you're a kid.

Remember the feeling? You gain a whole year on your friends in just one day. They stay four or seven or three, but you go to bed as a five-year-old and wake up the next morning a big boy of six.

It's a special day and should be carefully planned.

Those sentiments came through loud and clear from my son Jesse when he went from formerly five to solidly six. He wanted a birthday party at a certain place, with certain friends, a certain menu, a certain type of birthday cake, and certainly gifts.

Jesse's not the type of kid to spout off a list of gifts a mile long. True, he does have every aisle at Toys "R" Us committed to memory, but he is very thoughtful about his choice of potential presents.

So when I asked him what he wanted for his sixth birthday, I expected a well-planned reply. I was ready for suggestions like (1) a baseball glove [aisle six below the batting helmets], (2) Stomper 4x4 trucks [aisle seventeen next to the GI Joe remote-controlled tanks], or (3) Parcheesi board game [games are alphabetical in aisle one...between Pac-Man and Payday].

However, I did not get any of those answers. I was given a lesson in love instead.

"Dad, I'd like a ball to play with for my birthday," was Jesse's carefully planned reply.

"Great," I responded. "What kind of ball do you want?"

"I think I'd like a football or a soccer ball."

"Okay," I agreed but pressed him further. "Which would you like more, a football or a soccer ball?"

"Well...," he mused.

I should have known by his pause that it was coming.

"Well…if you had some time to play ball with me this next year, I'd really like a football for you and me to throw around in the backyard. But if you're gonna be real busy again, maybe you just better get me a soccer ball, because I can play soccer with the rest of the kids in the neighborhood."

He paused again. The silence was deafening.

"Uh…well…okay, buddy…I will…uh…I will make a choice and uh…surprise you on your birthday."

"Great, Daddy. I love you."

I grabbed my wife and went into another room to relay the conversation that had just transpired. It was as I was retelling the story that my son's real message came through.

He wasn't longing for the gifts.

He was longing for the giver.

It took an almost-six-year-old to remind me that relationships are more important than things.

Amazing story. Nothing would give me greater pleasure than to follow it up with something like *And so I played catch with my son in the backyard every day and never missed an opportunity to be there for him!*

Before you think I included this story just to throw heaping piles of guilt on your head, allow me to clarify. There's no question in my mind regarding that day as a defining moment in my life. As a result of that incident, I vowed to spend more time with my family and, in doing so, to live a more well-balanced life.

But some days were better than others. Before much time passed, I became too busy again. I became distracted by things that appeared important at the time but really were far less significant. I guess what I am trying to say is this: I'd hate to tell you how many more footballs I had to buy my son during his childhood and adolescence.

Life has a way of resisting our decisions. Circumstances change. We end one season of life and begin another. We change jobs. Or move. Or have to tend to an elderly parent. Or we're forced to spend ten weeks with our foot in a cast. For whatever reasons, life keeps changing. So we must change along with it. Balance demands our attention day by day, year by year, throughout each and every stage of life.

Will you do it? Are you willing to make the commitment to lead a balanced life, knowing that along with that commitment is the understanding that you will go with the flow as life's river changes in current, flow, depth, and direction? Sure, there will be times when you feel as if you're paddling upstream. There will be seasons when you feel as though you can't fight the current.

But the work is worth it. You are making a stand for the things and people that are truly important in your life.

Let's conclude with the metaphor with which we began. I don't want to think of you rolling around in the cinders at the 330-yard mark. I want to think of you making your way *confidently* around the track and crossing the finish line, having run the race you intended to run. I want to see your coach waiting for you at the finish line, telling you that you've run well.

The only way that is going to happen is if you get serious about the issues we've been discussing.

Pursue and practice Priorities.

Get serious about Attention, Connection, and Reflection.

Pursue and practice Endurance.

Get serious about Forecasting, Focus, and Fun.

Pursue and practice Pacing.

Get serious about Learning, Labor, and Leisure.

You may have to start small and work your way up, but at least you'll be making a start. When these pursuits start happening, this message becomes more than just some pages in that book you read on an otherwise boring airplane trip. It's life changing. And that's good stuff.

Notes

1. Karen S. Peterson, "There's No Way to Beat the Clock," *USA Today,* April 13, 1989, 1D.

2. Amby Burfoot and Bill Billing Jr., "The Perfect Pace," *Runner's World,* November 1985, 39.

3. Richard Nelson Bolles, *The Three Boxes of Life and How to Get Out of Them: An Introduction to Life/Work Planning* (Berkeley, CA: Ten Speed Press, 1978), 5–10.

About the Author

Bill Butterworth's extraordinary ability to blend humor, storytelling, wisdom, and practicality has made him one of the most sought-after corporate speakers throughout North America. Through his wit, warmth, insight, and realism, he brings help and hope to audiences everywhere.

Bill taught at the college level for thirteen years and was a counselor for six years prior to his current passion for motivating men and women in the workplace. He was awarded the Hal Holbrook Award by the International Platform Association, whose past and present members include Mark Twain, Theodore Roosevelt, Bob Hope, and Elizabeth Dole. Bill is one of the select few members to be named a top-rated speaker by the association.

Since 1988, Bill has traveled full time, speaking to hundreds of audiences as small as eighteen and as large as eighteen thousand. His Fortune 500 clients include:

Allstate	Citibank
American Express	DaimlerChrysler
Bank of America	First Data Corporation
BlueCross BlueShield	Ford Motor Company
Boise Cascade	Hilton Hotels
Century 21 Real Estate	Johnson Controls

MassMutual	T. Rowe Price
Parker Hannifin	Verizon
PNC Bank	Wachovia Bank
SBC	Walt Disney Company

Bill has also addressed twenty-six of the teams in the National Football League as well as more than a dozen teams in Major League Baseball. Bill's complete client list reads like a who's who of corporations, associations, educational agencies, and professional sports teams.

In 2004 Bill established the Butterworth Communicators Institute (BCI) to help train men and women to find their speaking voice and raise their speaking ability to the next level. The overwhelmingly positive response to BCI has been gratifying as students maximize their skills through this intensive yet intimate three-day workshop.

In addition to the On-the-Fly series, Bill has written more than a dozen books, including *The Promise of the Second Wind* and *When Life Doesn't Turn Out Like You Planned.*

For more information about Bill Butterworth, please visit his Web site at www.BillButterworth.com.